BOTTOM FISHING

BOTTOM
FISHING

FRANK WOOLNER
and
HENRY LYMAN

Nick Lyons Books
Winchester Press
The Salt Water Sportsman Library

Produced by
NICK LYONS BOOKS
31 West 21st St.
New York, NY 10011

Published and distributed by
WINCHESTER PRESS
New Century Publishers, Inc.
220 Old New Brunswick Road
Piscataway, NJ 08854

PRINTED IN THE UNITED STATES OF AMERICA
10 9 8 7 6 5 4 3 2

Designed by Tasha Hall

Library of Congress Cataloging in Publication Data

Woolner, Frank, 1916-
    Bottom fishing.

    Includes index.
    1. Bottom fishing. I. Lyman, Henry, 1915-
II. Title.
SH455.6.W66   1984   799.1'6   84-1061
ISBN 0-8329-0363-9

CONTENTS

ACKNOWLEDGMENTS

Fishermen often express wonder concerning our writing efforts, not over what is finally produced, but over what our methods may be. Where does Lyman leave off and Woolner begin—and vice versa? We have been writing as a team for so many years that there is no pat answer. However, the basic plan is simple enough: One selects a topic in which he may have a little more expertise than the other, pounds out a rough draft, submits it to his coauthor, who then tears it apart like a barracuda worrying a mullet. The final copy therefore ends up as a sort of compromise—and each of us must acknowledge the help of the other.

Two people cannot possibly know all there is to know about any aspect of marine angling, so what you read in this book does not come solely from two individuals, nor from what totals more than a century of our fishing experiences. We have picked the brains and writings of our fellow outdoor scribes over a long period of years and are indebted to them for a mass of information salted away in our memories or files. If any one of them reads in what follows something that he thinks was his own idea, it undoubtedly is. We stole it! Although we may be considered editorial thieves, our thanks are nonetheless sincere.

Add to the informational chowder countless scraps and pieces supplied by readers of *Salt Water Sportsman,* and by those we have met afloat and ashore in our angling travels. In many cases, names were not known and even faces have faded to a hazy blur, yet each made some contribution to this volume. Wherever they may be today, our gratitude is with them.

The staff of *Salt Water Sportsman,* fishermen all, deserves particular recognition. When in doubt concerning some fine point on tackle, methods, or rigs, we have turned to them for help and have accepted their advice gladly. Particular thanks go to Editor Barry Gibson, charter skipper of the *Shark II* operating out of Boothbay Harbor, Maine. Barry waded through our draft manuscript and made many suggestions that were incorporated into its final form. His artist wife Jean did noble work in interpreting our rough sketches to produce the line drawings that are found throughout the book.

Finally, our thanks to Nick Lyons, fisherman and author in his own right, who is responsible for getting this volume into print. He has been very patient.

one

DOWN TO PAY
DIRT

*E*xperienced anglers who have, like the Devil, journeyed up and down across the world, and back and forth in it, forever raise impolite eyebrows when less knowledgeable colleagues dismiss bottom fishing as an amateur's game. Quite naturally, a beginner is apt to be ham-handed at first encounter with a vast and perplexing sea, plus tackle with which he is unfamiliar. By the same token, folk who leap straight into marine combat with artificial lures are quite as inept during a period of basic training that always precedes graduation at the head of the class.

It has long been our firm belief that, regardless of a sportsman's eventual preference as to method, his education is sadly neglected without an initial cram course in the hoodwinking of fish down deep, on natural bait or jigs. Like the country kid who launches a lifetime of pleasure with a birch pole and a gob of angleworms, to finally master a dry fly in fast water, early days provide indispensable knowledge about the habits of a given quarry.

True, it is quite possible to attain a small measure of success by dumping a mismatched bottom rig into the brine and, with a mite of

1

silent prayer, to luck into an occasional prize. However, as one learns the subtle nuances of presentation one's success ratio soars. The technique is a supreme challenge, certainly one of the first angling methods used by man, and surely one of the most demanding.

Therefore, belay any suspicion that bottom fishing is less than high art. Among our friends we admire many who are skilled in each of the disciplines yet derive greatest satisfaction in outwitting a wary trophy cruising in blue depths. We have reason to believe it well nigh impossible to master modern sport fishing without truly understanding this technique.

The game is truly as old as Kipling's everlasting hills, for fishing gear is regularly discovered in the middens of Stone-Age man. In Latin America, lost tribes of Indians predating the Incas fashioned lines of twisted hemp, with cleverly designed stone sinkers and hooks made from thorns, hammered copper, and the teeth of both land animals and sea creatures. It is likely that early man harvested the sea for sustenance rather than for sport, but there must have been smiles of pure pleasure on bronzed faces as glittering fishes resisted the hand-over-hand battle.

The sport as we know it may date back to Aelian in the third century, for his description of a fly made from red wool and wax-colored saddle hackle appears to be the first mention of an artificial lure. Rods, crude prototypes of the magnificent shafts now available, were certainly in use by the middle of the seventeenth century—and quite possibly well before that time. Dame Juliana Berners has been credited with listing a number of fly patterns as early as 1406.

In any event, there is little doubt that bottom-bouncing has always been a primary means of extracting fishes from the sea. Although probably predated by the spear, the hook, line, and sinker have forever intrigued more of earth's people than all artificial lures combined. There is magic in the business, tranquillity, a sense of achievement, perhaps something of an addictive lottery.

To clinch the matter, consider a fact of life grudgingly admitted by the finest of fly casters, trollers, and enthusiastic flingers of lures. We hate to admit as much, yet there are frustrating times when it is absolutely necessary to employ natural bait—or go hungry while our neighbors rack up impressive catches. Moreover, a number of much sought-after species—because of their feeding habits or mouth structure—are rarely goaded into taking a simulation of the real thing. Sure, it is possible to boat a tautog on a small lead-head jig or fly, but this is surely one of those exceptions to prove a rule. We have tempted the odd winter flounder on a miniature metal jig, but that's not the swiftest way to stock a deep-freeze unit with tender fillet of sole.

Obviously, all fish eat natural forage in order to survive, and it doesn't matter whether the species is a gargantuan bluefin tuna or a tiny-mite exotic hovering over tropical coral heads. They eat, but we must give them what they desire, and it is necessary to understand that many are extremely selective.

Gilly Cunningham, happy with a husky codfish—proof that bottom fishing appeals to anglers of all ages.

Pacific halibut is a prize catch off the California coast and hugs the bottom closely.

Mullet are prime examples: You can take them with a meticulous presentation of green peas, of all things; on doughballs prepared with a mixture of imagination and faith; on single, small angleworms. In Pacific waters, roughly from Monterey southward into Baja, the opaleye grazes on gobs of a certain moss but will also take store-bought green peas. For some surprising reason, Atlantic winter flounders are enthusiastic about whole-kernel corn. Peas and corn do not grow on the ocean's bottom, but this fodder is accepted, often greedily. You can chum with it, often a most effective stratagem, or you can bait with it.

Long, long ago Atlantic Coast striped bass fishermen chummed with ground-up lobsters and also used this gourmet's delight as bait. High cost of living prohibits modern repetition, yet it is possible to work a gimmick at no cost. If you know an amiable restaurateur, see if he will save for you the discarded shells and leavings from lobster dinners. Smashed up and dumped into the water as a chum slick, such shells can be day-savers—organic, so no pollution is involved.

Barry Gibson decks a cod that fell for a synthetic tube lure fished deep.

Note that there is a marine form of "match the hatch," although it is far from the inland fly caster's exact simulation of a specific insect. Briefly, one must often use or simulate a bait that is in glut and happens to be favored by selective game fishes on a given ground.

It is generally agreed that *Homo sapiens* has more brains than any fish, yet we often only think we know better—and thus casually ignore the sharply imprinted patterns of natural selection. Instinct is the word most often used in this context, although its precise meaning requires a smidgen of fancy footwork in definition. Almost certainly there are imprinted genes and mores that influence each organism. There is evidence of memory.

The creatures of land and sea are rightly afraid of that greatest of earth's predators, man, and therefore they develop increasing wariness as they are hunted down. You can catch Bahamas bonefish one after another, since on remote flats the white fox is not excessively spooky. Greater finesse is required on the Florida keys where a sloppy cast will send every bonefish racing off like an animated torpedo.

It has been demonstrated that certain fishes are capable of learning. How long they retain memory is anybody's guess, yet it may be for longer periods than we think. That ingrown terror can be overcome by conditioning is not questioned. One can "train" dockside species to arrive en masse by rattling a net loaded with foodstuffs, or by flashing a color they have been taught to associate with a dinner hour. These are no meanderings of unscientific conjecture: All have been proven beyond a vestige of doubt.

However, except in controlled situations, a bottom-bouncer encounters the wildest of wild fishes, which are endowed with natural caution and must be brought to account through guile. In forthcoming pages we intend to examine many of the tactics evolved to accomplish a pleasant end result. Although the human mind is far more devious than that of lesser creatures, there are times when we accord the quarry more ability to reason than it is due—and thus strike out through failure to respect a fish's sensitive nerve ends. Whether it is instinct, reflex action, or a memory bank, the fish often seem to know when a thing is wrong—and the larger a game fish grows, the more highly developed its natural caution.

Admittedly, all hands roll collective eyes to heaven when, rarely, a world's-record monster is caught by some beginner on his first trip to the salt! This has happened more often than regulars like to admit, yet it still remains an exception. Entertain no doubt on this score. Well-educated rod handlers take a majority of trophies, just as scientifically taught fresh-water anglers bag more respectable trout than the proverbial barefoot boy with his bent pin and tomato can full of garden worms. Over a long haul, no amateur is likely to best a man or woman who knows precisely how to operate. Knowledge is not acquired without study, expertise in the handling of professionally matched tackle, and a turtle's age spent unraveling the secrets of the sea.

One must strive to understand the life-style of each species sought, its optimum season on the grounds, its degree of selectivity, and usual feeding habits. Luck is for dreamers: Success crowns the brows of people who have polished approach and execution to that point where the competition expresses admiration by declaring: "By Tophet, the guy *thinks* like a fish!"

All of the signs are there after an angler has become keen enough to

Small boat liveries and privately owned craft are favored by bottom fishermen on all coasts in sheltered waters.

read subtle hints; to assess bottom conformation best suited to serve as marine highways and banquet tables; to tuck away in convoluted brain cells valuable information about rips that develop at various stages of tidal ebb and flow. While gnarled and ancient sea dogs are fond of declaring that nobody hits pay dirt without wetting a line, a regular on site invariably reserves his or her share of stamina for the calculated hours of greatest promise. A muscular lad in his twenties may be perfectly capable of working around the clock, yet he is unlikely to do any better than a cagey old-timer who chooses timing of his shots with infinite care.

Local conditions must be figured into the equation. On one stretch of coast, wind from a specific direction will blow bait shoreward with game fishes in close pursuit; on another strand, breezes from an exactly opposite quarter enhance the odds. Offshore, or in sheltered bays, today's sophisticated graph recorders trace exact pictures of structures most likely to provide sport and, in many instances, spy out and report on the fishes themselves.

Granted, Murphy's Law applies on the grounds—as elsewhere. Frequently one will be discouraged by "dirt in the water," a messy accumulation of drifting weed or the so-called goglum created by a concentration of algae bloom. If this garbage is thick enough to hamper practical bottom fishing, one simply marks time in the hope that a scouring change of tide will sweep this stuff out to far horizons. At night, one often encounters "fire in the water," billions of tiny, light-emitting Dinoflagellata that can make every line, leader, and bait glow with cold flame. The ill effect is partially defeated by use of fine diameter monofilament.

Ideally, night or day, you are going to be fishing with a reasonably taut line extending from rod tip to an anchored bait. Among minor plagues there may be a measure of wind-belly and/or current-belly, which requires rather constant tending. From shore, when bites are few and far between, a sand spike makes sense—yet a hand-held rod is always most efficient. Gunwale-mounted holders serve a similar purpose offshore, again never as surefire and sensitive to response as the handhold, yet quite adequate if an angler doesn't get bored and repair to the cabin for a mug of hot coffee and a tall-tale session when the sea appears to be a biological desert.

Among tenacious myths befogging the concept of bottom fishing, one sometimes notes a curious tendency to use gear that is heavier than actually needed. This is an error, for to operate with overkill bulk detracts from the joy of angling and also handicaps presentation. Unquestionably there is a place for just about every heft of matched rod, reel, line, and terminal rig, depending on the size of species sought, depth to be plumbed with bait or lure, and technique arbitrarily imposed.

For general bottom fishing we lean toward the revolving spool combination, yet millions of highly successful anglers do remarkably well with spinning tackle. Actually, there is nothing wrong with fixed spool where baits are offered in relatively shallow depths. Spinning tackle is *not* advisable in deep water, say anything over 50 feet straight down, or where subsurface currents are strong. There, a conventional bay or trolling rig proves more efficient because the reel offers brute strength, ensures a maximum of control, stores an adequate supply of Dacron braid (which doesn't stretch like monofilament), and usually

Hal Lyman waits at the edge of a tidal rip for winter flounder.

is geared down to take hard cracking in stride.

In high surf the situation changes, for casting then becomes an essential first hurdle. Basic conventional squidding reels and open-faced spinning types prevent undue swearing when one must lob bait and sinker well beyond three or four cresting waves that are marching shoreward. Here, too, unless waters are unusually calm, a long rod is preferable to a short one, both to facilitate throwing to maximum distance, and because its 10- to 11-foot overall length keeps running line above tumbling, clutching breakers.

To a great extent, each tackle combination is geared to its task and to a species sought. There are magnificent crazies who hunt giant sharks from shore, drifting huge baits off the beach under breakaway floats, inflated garbage bags, or balloons. These monster hunters rarely "go light": They commonly employ what amounts to big-game tackle, bucket-sized reels, and 80- to 130-pound test line.

Of course this is a highly specialized sport and is not in the bailiwick of the multitudes who favor practical conventional and spinning gear. The key word is *practical* and explains the reason why an ardent bottom-bouncer invariably invests in several tackle combinations. There isn't much fun catching two-pound winter flounders on a rig designed to out-muscle a corpulent channel bass or black drum. There may be questionable "sport" in wrestling big cod off a deep-sea floor with spinning gear, but fishing companions hunched over party-boat railings will fare far better with conventional equipment and the less elastic Dacron lines.

Deep-down bottom fishing is most often practiced from the decks of party boats or private vessels of considerable size, seaworthy enough to visit the offshore banks, wrecks, reefs, and rockpiles—yet far more baited hooks are guided into relatively shoal water close to shore. There are a few notable exceptions: In Hawaii, cliff-hanging adventurers use a form of anchored trolley line to present big baits to huge ulua cruising in considerable depths just outside a steep inshore dropoff. Trolley lines are also employed on a number of coastal piers along the Atlantic seaboard.

For all practical purposes there are four basic weapons systems employed by dedicated bottom fishermen. One is the hand line, still favored in remote areas of the world. In the backcountry of Latin America, native fishermen utilize—and mighty skillfully—a length of fairly heavy monofilament wrapped around an empty beer can. The cast is a mixture of aboriginal heave-and-haul, plus a crude application of spinning. Whirling bait and sinker to throw, the can is extended horizontally so that the mono peels off just as it would from a classic spinning reel. In retrieve, line is swiftly rewound on the can. Sounds complicated, but nimble natives are masters of the art.

Perhaps one rung higher on a ladder of sophistication, a surprising number of backcountry specialists from South Carolina down through Florida to the Gulf of Mexico, people often well versed in the use of ultramodern equipment, still rely on the ancient bamboo-cane pole with a short length of line knotted to its limber tip. Practitioners declare that this is the best of all gear with which to harvest finicky nibblers like eastern sheepshead and mullet.

For the utmost in sport, however, rod and reel reigns supreme. Weapons systems are about equally divided between revolving spool and spinning, with rods ranging all the way from ultralight fixed spool, through bait-casting tackle, to popping rods, to the true high surf stick—and beyond that to far huskier, shorter offshore rods and

Until the tide is right and the smelt arrive, it is a waiting game—and a cold one!

reels designed to winch up any "engine block with a wiggle."

It is even possible to use a fly rod in sheltered waters, although the long wand is seldom as efficient in the presentation of a bottom bait as are the conventional and fixed-spool rigs. Fitted with ring guides instead of the usual snakes, a fly rod can be worth its salt for drifting sea worms or shrimps down through an inlet on a falling tide, or for presenting these tidbits in a chum slick to entice schooling weakfish. The technique was once popular but is now seldom employed because spinning does the job better.

There is still a measure of "purism" in bottom fishing—at least to the extent that individual anglers often settle on catching one or two species to the practical exclusion of all else. This zero-in approach is apparent, for example, where striped bass, red drum, bluefish, and pompano are deemed most desirable. Yet there are hosts of happy warriors who feel close to paradise only when deep-baiting pot-bellied northern cod or the stubborn groupers of more southerly waters. Count it likely that a majority of these single-track people have done their homework in studying (and catching) just about every locally available species. While preferring to narrow down and take dead aim at one or two favorites, they are, in every sense of the word, *advanced* anglers.

Since every fish feeds on some sort of natural fodder, and many are close to omnivorous, the dedicated bottom-bouncer is sure to come up with a share of unwanted customers. Certain tricks of the trade help to defeat party poopers, yet be assured that a deep-down offering will be inhaled by such interlopers as dogfish, skates, and sea robins. No matter. Artfully prepared, all of the three are perfectly edible—a fact providing small consolation to a red-hot rod pilot who bewails losing carefully rigged baits to critters he regards as trash. When skates, for

This boccacio (or salmon grouper) is just one of a wide variety of rockfish available to Southern California anglers who fish offshore over submerged rocky structures in water from 200 to over 1000 feet deep. Boccacio are considered to be the best eating of all the rockfish by some; however, most specimens average a bit smaller than the brute in this photo.

example, hug bottom after munching on a tasty tidbit intended for a prized game fish, tempers fray and—all too often—frustrated anglers kill and discard everything, regarded collectively as "lesser breeds without the law." However, no matter how aggravating these frequently abundant spoilers can be, it is better to release them uninjured on the correct premise that every living creature in the world ocean fills an ecological niche.

No matter where one seeks fun and relaxation—at the edge of the big pond or out where ground swells may dictate Dramamine—bottom fishing is far more likely to boost a success ratio than slavish dedication to artificial lures alone. Gentlemen Rankers who declare the method boring when compared to operating with flies, plugs,

Blowfish, often eaten with relish as "Sea Squab" in the mid-Atlantic coastal area, can be poisonous in more southern waters. The tail and strips of flesh along the backbone only are cooked. Liver and roe should be avoided in any waters.

metal squids, or trolled hardware cannot have savored that almost indescribable sensation of imminent warfare as a running line twitches, suddenly tightens, and then begins to spool off at increasing speed.

Although this climactic and portentous moment has been preceded by skillful delivery to a suspected payoff area, a fisherman grits his teeth, squints his eyes, and goes rigid with tension. The mind clicks over rapidly, for it is necessary to guess just what is happening down in darkling depths and to set a hook at precisely the right moment. Imagination heightens suspense, for until solidly tied into a respectable prize, until you feel writhing weight and power, no assessment is possible. Illogically, perhaps almost madly at this moment of initial contact, you are absolutely convinced that an IGFA record-breaker has made a final, fatal mistake.

Larry Green of San Francisco admires two lingcod he caught on bait in the depths.

two

MEANS TO AN END

*T*he basic ploy when bottom fishing is to present food to a fish where it may gobble it down with a minimum of search and effort. The fundamental method of accomplishing this is to lower a baited hook to the ocean floor with the help of an added weight and then wait for the fish to arrive on the scene. Known as still fishing, it is one of the most primitive methods of angling, yet it is also today an extremely popular way of bringing fish from the sea to the table. It has one great advantage: It gets results!

Still fishing may be done from boats of any size; from bridges, docks, piers, and floats; even from bluffs and rocky headlands that extend out into an estuary or into the ocean itself. Although the technique is simple, it will vary according to the species sought, the waters fished, and environmental factors such as currents, winds, and type of bottom. Some fundamental rules apply everywhere.

The first of these is the necessity to match terminal tackle to the fishing conditions, always assuming the rod, reel, and line are already matched for the job at hand. For example, a one-ounce sinker will not take a two-ounce chunk of mullet to the bottom when a four-knot current is running. On the other hand, if a six-ounce sinker is used when the bait is a tiny piece of sea worm weighing less than a half ounce, chances of feeling a nibble are greatly reduced. For almost all still fishing except under unusual circumstances, the rule of thumb is that the sinker weight should be at least twice the weight of the baited hook. If currents are strong, the ratio will have to be increased until the sinker itself holds firmly on bottom.

Another general rule, which has a good many exceptions, is that any bait used should cover as much of the metal as is practical while presenting that bait in a natural manner. It is usually possible to bury the entire hook from eye to point in a squid or similar large offering, but when this is done, the hook's point and barb may fail to make contact with the jaws of the potential catch even if it swallows hook and all deep into its gullet. When strain comes on the line, the fish will then spit out its free meal and swim away unscathed. With tough baits, leave the entire barb and at least a part of the bend exposed. With softer ones such as shucked clams, this may not be necessary—

The Larry Greens of San Francisco have a light tackle ball with pile perch.

and there is an advantage to hiding all metal which might alarm the fish.

A notable exception to the rule of covering hook metal is when live bait is used. It will stop being alive almost immediately if steel is forced through a major portion of its anatomy. In baits ranging from anchovies to mackerel, the hook point should be forced through the lips, the upper jaw, the flesh just back of the head or just in front of the dorsal fin. If minnow types used are chunky, as in the case of butterfish, many anglers prefer to place the hook just *behind* the dorsal. Live crabs should be hooked at the rear of the carapace; shrimps, just behind the eyes or at the base of the tail. Do not penetrate a dark-colored vital area.

With baits that are long and wiggly—the various sea worms and the pile worm—they may remain alive or not. In most cases when still fishing, it is advisable to have the forward end of the worm lying straight along the hook shank and the remainder streaming out naturally back of the hook bend. This will produce a wiggle even in the slightest current whether the critter is alive or dead. However, if the worms are small or have been broken into pieces, several may have to be jammed onto the hook to form an enticing gob. They will still take fish, particularly the true bottom browsers such as Atlantic winter flounder. Soft-lipped flounders in general have an aggravating habit of nipping off the end of streamed baits and thus avoiding the hook entirely.

Many, ourselves included, prefer long-shanked hooks when still fishing for species such as these same flounders, surf perches, and the like. There is no danger of the soft-mouthed quarry biting through the leader, but chances are better than even that a short-shanked model would be swallowed. Even long-nosed pliers will not recover the hook sometimes, and minor surgery is required to do the job. The long shank is rarely gobbled down in its entirety. Giving that exposed long shank a coat of red fingernail polish will enhance its value as an attractor to the fish. When a good deal of any hook is exposed, use of gold- or cadmium-plated styles is recommended for the same purpose.

We have never been enthusiastic about use of flashers or spinners to act as attractors when still fishing because, unless there is a strong current running, they tend to drop to the bottom and tangle with leaders and hooks. However, other devices can improve catches.

Trophy Virginia red drum (channel bass) beached on a whole mullet bait.

Colored plastic skirts placed over the eye of a hook at the point where it is connected to the leader, particularly when whole bait fish is used, often brings more strikes than the minnow alone. Colored beads serve the same purpose. A float, which often has a fluorescent paint finish, rigged on a leader several inches ahead of the hook serves as an attractor, adds action to the bait, and also keeps it off the bottom where crabs and other scavengers are apt to munch on it. One specialized float, christened years ago as the Jersey Doodlebug, looks much like a fresh-water fly-rod popping bug with the buoyant material molded onto the shank of the hook itself. It is effective when you're after small species and may be sweetened by adding a bait strip to it.

A final still fishing rule that might be termed a command is to use fresh bait whenever possible. If you can legally catch or dig your own right on the grounds, so much the better. A squid that is turning pink, a menhaden that shades toward yellow, or a sardine that is starting to resemble a dead olive leaf is a bait of desperation. Your nose normally may be the best indicator of what is fresh and what is not. Make use of it.

While using an anchored boat or a fixed shore structure as a fishing platform, as is the case when still fishing, there is another method that will take many bottom feeders. Termed jigging, it involves the use of a lure, normally of bright metal, which is lowered to the bottom, reeled in a foot or two, then given action by raising the rod tip smartly and lowering it again. The process is repeated time and time again until a fish is hooked or the angler gives up.

Jigging in deep water—40 feet to several hundred—was developed originally by commercial fishermen using handlines. Scandinavians were among the first to use this method widely back in the early 1800s. The Norway, or Viking, jig, which may weigh as much as 24 ounces and which has the general shape of a streamlined lamb chop, is still popular on all coasts among sport fishermen. Today's jigs are usually chrome plated, may have a swivel molded into the head of the lure, and are armed with either treble or single hooks, whether or not they have a swivel. The odd shape of these jigs gives them a fluttering action when the rod tip is lowered. Hooks may be sweetened with a bit

Typical charter boats equipped for all types of angling at Wellfleet, Cape Cod, Massachusetts.

of natural bait if desired.

In the Northeast, party-boat skippers prefer an eight-ounce dia-mond jig which, as the name implies, is in the shape of a diamond in cross section. They also prefer a fixed treble hook to a swiveled single. Although these trebles tend to foul bottom, when fishing is fast the boat's mate can unhook the catches quickly so that the angler can get his lure back in the water with a minimum of delay. Move farther south on the Atlantic Coast area, however, and the Nordic jig with a single hook predominates. Success ratio appears to be the reason. Homemade pipe jigs, described in detail in another chapter, are used extensively on the Pacific side—primarily because they are easily and cheaply made. Undoubtedly they will become more popular elsewhere as word of their economy spreads.

When deep jigging in waters up to about a hundred feet, the lure is often tied directly to 30- to 50-pound test monofilament line. The size of the jig itself prevents even toothed species from cutting themselves free. However, mono in waters greater than that depth is not practical because it has too much stretch. This makes setting the hook difficult. The stretch is also a handicap when trying to snap a jig free from some underwater obstruction. Braided Dacron of 50 to 80 pounds is the usual choice—and this requires use of a leader to decrease visibility. Regular wire is not recommended: It tends to kink, then break as the lure is moved up and down regularly. Nylon-covered cable will serve, particularly if the species sought, like snappers or groupers, makes a habit of heading for their rock or coral hidey-holes when hooked. In most cases, about 15 feet of 100-pound test monofilament will prevent break-offs from normal causes. We are believers in minimal hardware on terminal tackle and recommend splicing leader and line together rather than using a swivel or other connector.

Jigging is not confined to deep water. Lures as light as a quarter ounce may be used with success in the shallows on species ranging from weakfish to Pacific rockfish. Obviously tackle and lures should match the fish sought. A rod with a soft or weepy tip, favored by some who cast very light lures or small natural baits, is not good for jigging. Not only is more energy used to move the lure because the rod tip flexes through a wide arc, but also setting the hook is difficult when the strike comes because the lure flutters toward bottom. Graphite and boron models have more resilience than glass and should be the choice if your pocketbook can stand it. A free-spool reel is preferred over a spinning model because it gives greater control over a jigged lure and a hooked fish.

Monofilament line is satisfactory for most light jigging with lures weighing up to a couple of ounces. Above that weight, pick Dacron because of its minimal stretch mentioned earlier. Note, however, that a leader is a good investment no matter what type of line is used. Since the lures are small, fish may well take them down into the gullet, and even a 20-pound line will be chafed through on teeth or jaws.

During recent years, a rapid advance in the technology of electronics has benefited sport fishermen. Highly efficient graph recorders, sometimes called "fishfinders," are now priced well within the sometimes limited budgets of everyday anglers. Now universally accepted as primary aids—not so long ago referred to as magic boxes—these

A print-out from a Lowrance X-15 recording fishfinder shows two concentrations of fish. The dark concentration on the left peak was predominantly squid; the fish to the right were cod.

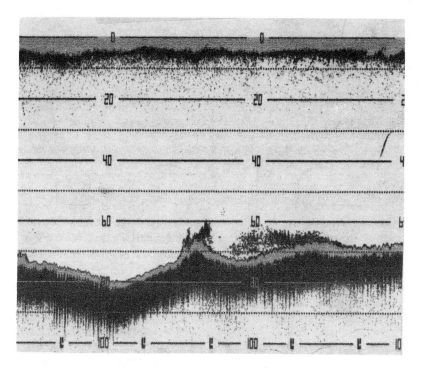

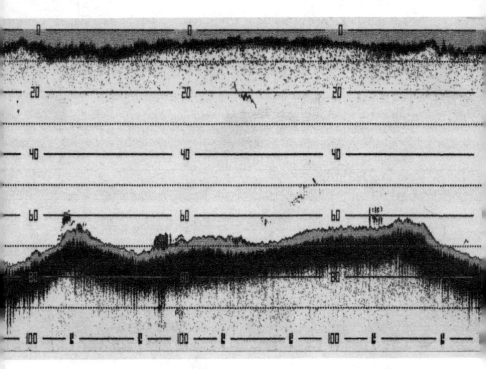

Several concentrations of fish appear on this print-out from a Lowrance X-15 recording fishfinder. To the left is a mixed bag of squid and cod; to its right, a bait concentration, probably squid. Slightly more to the right is a sparse school of bait up from the bottom. Above that, one of two fish were up high, near the 20-foot mark. Further right is a marking that probably is caused by long strands of kelp, or possibly bait. Note the single fish to the right of the last marking at the 70-foot level.

tools accurately record bottom contours and depth; they are capable of locating schools or even individual game fishes cruising at various depths. An effective recorder automatically reduces the ancient problems associated with dead reckoning, range marking, and plain guess-and-by-god prospecting for lucrative ground. As of this writing, one is unlikely to find any sport fishing craft larger than, say arbitrarily, an outboard skiff up to 14 feet in length, without sophisticated electronics. However, lacking such a boon to pinpoint positioning, tried-and-true methods continue to bring results.

Unless a particular hot spot has been pinpointed by taking cross bearings on fixed shore-based objects, boat fishermen may have trouble locating fish just by anchoring as the spirit moves. Drifting is the answer. Without an anchor down, the craft will be carried along by wind and current so that baited hooks will move over the bottom to new areas where the quarry may lurk. When a strike comes, do not drop the anchor immediately. Play the fish, then, using either oars or motor, move upwind or against the current, well above the spot where the fish has been located, before making the drop. Depth of water is the key to the distance moved. A rule of thumb is to treble the water depth prior to anchoring. For example, if 30 feet of water is under the keel, steam a minimum of 90 feet against wind or current, then drop the anchor.

In the case of some species such as tautog (blackfish) the strike area may be extremely small. An underwater cavern or rock formation is the place the fish calls home and it may not venture far from this ideal feeding ground. By anchoring well above this spot, you can make minor adjustments for proper distance simply by letting out more anchor line. It is better to err on the side of too much distance than too little.

In many cases, drifting with no use of the anchor at all gets best results. Flatfishes, for example, may be feeding over a wide stretch of sandy or muddy bottom. Still fishing will bring hits from only a comparatively small area. Drifting brings the bait to the fish rather than forcing them to come to the bait. Since the ocean floor varies as the boat moves from place to place, it is well to "feel for bottom"— that is, to test depths at frequent intervals. When the sinker hits, reel in enough line so that it will not foul; drift a few minutes, then repeat the process.

Wind and current strength, of course, influence the speed of drift. At times either force, or the combination of both, will make it nearly impossible to keep a hook close to the bottom without the use of sinkers too heavy to be practical. If the anchor, snubbed short so that it just touches bottom without catching firmly, is lowered, excessive speed can be checked. A better trick, however, is to use a burlap bag partially filled with sand or small rocks in place of the anchor. The sack will not foul readily, yet will slow the drift sufficiently to allow easy fishing.

Another problem arises when wind and current are moving in opposite directions. Then the boat may remain almost stationary with no drift at all. Often this may be corrected by shifting trim. Moving weights, such as an outboard motor gasoline can, from one spot to another can make the difference. The easiest weight to shift is yourself or your companions. Always keeping safety afloat in mind, move forward or aft to let wind or current take over.

Because drifting in reality is a type of slow trolling, a much wider choice of baits, lures, and combinations of both may be used when you are still fishing. A fluttering strip of fish belly, squid, or any other natural offering can be a killer. In still fishing, with some exceptions, the sinker usually is mounted below the hook or hooks. When drifting, better results are obtained by having the sinker ahead of the hook. Sliding egg sinkers, threaded on the line and kept in place by a swivel at the end of the leader, are an excellent choice for this type of presentation. A strike is relayed up the line to the rod tip immediately and the fish itself does not feel the full weight of the sinker when it bites.

Spinners and some of the smaller flashers are activated as a boat moves through the water while drifting. These should be placed at least six inches ahead of the baited hook for best results. A host of bucktail-type jigs and metal squids can be put to good use without any sinker at all on a drift. Jigging any of these on or near bottom as the craft moves will entice species ranging from toothed flounders to semitropical grunts, groupers, and snappers. Some fishermen add the sliding sinker mentioned above when they wish to go deep. We prefer simply to use a heavier lure for better control of the whole terminal rig.

Taking powers of any lures used in this manner are increased by adding a bit of bait to the hook, usually in the form of a strip that flutters. Plastic worms and the variously colored plastic curlicue-type dressings now available also work well. Note that plastic is slightly buoyant, which can be an advantage if the lure has to travel over rough bottom where it may foul readily. If you want to have the lure hug the ocean floor when drifting over sand bars and mud flats, choose pork-rind strips, which sink quickly. These may be purchased with a tail hook mounted in them to outwit fish that strike short.

On the Pacific Coast, the term *mooching* has developed for a type of fishing that now escapes exact definition. Several books and countless articles have been written on the art of mooching, but unfortunately modern authors cannot agree on just what is involved. Originally the technique was developed for taking Pacific salmons. Tackle included a fairly limber six- to eight-foot rod mounting a free-spool reel. A crescent sinker was attached between line and leader, below that came a flasher or dodger, then a plug of herring cut to spin as it traveled through the water. The whole works was trolled slowly, fished in a current from an anchored boat, and drifted over the fishing grounds.

Although this technique is still widely used, what is now termed mooching is done for many bottom-fishing species including lingcod and rockfishes. West Coast old-timers may wince, yet the term now applies to many different methods that deviate widely from the original. Drifting with a sinker bumping bottom and trailed by a leader ending in a baited hook is considered mooching by many anglers. Similarly, fishing an artificial in the same manner, whether or not the lure is sweetened with a bit of bait, pork rind, or plastic, falls under the broad term *mooching.*

Perhaps because they have become infatuated with the word, some Pacific fishermen classify as mooching what is known on all other coasts as spin-jigging. As the name implies, spinning tackle is used with the rod about seven feet long and of rather stiff action. Line ranges from eight- to 12-pound test monofilament and the lure generally is of the bucktail type with the hook point riding upward so that it will not foul bottom. The platform is a drifting boat. The lure is cast up-current, then allowed to sink until it touches bottom. If the drift is rapid there is no need to retrieve and cast again on a regular basis—just give the jig a hopping action on a tight line by lifting and lowering the rod tip sharply. If the drift is slow, retrieve a little line each time the lure touches down, but keep the rate of retrieve moderate to slow at all times.

For reasons best known to the fish, strikes occur more frequently when the jig is heading back toward bottom than when it is being tweaked toward the surface. This technique can be very successful on many species including some of the glamour fish such as tarpon, which are not usually associated with bottom fishing.

Casting is also involved in several other types of bottom fishing. The most obvious of these is when working the surf. It is not within the scope of this book to go into the details of surf fishing, but a few general observations are in order. First, it is necessary to get the bait far enough away from the tide line to reach the spot where the fish may be feeding. Unless you have a friend on hand with a small helicopter to carry sinker and hook to sea, casting is the answer. In passing, we should mention that kites and small balloons have been tried from time to time to accomplish this purpose but have never achieved wide popularity because of the complexity of the gear involved and the fact that an offshore wind is a necessity.

Standard terminal tackle for such fishing is a three-way swivel with the line tied to one of the swivel eyes, a sinker with a short length of leader material to the next, and the hook, snelled (with a long piece of leader material attached), tied to the final eye. Note that the sinker is above hook and bait. The trouble with such a rig is that when the bait is picked up the fish feel the weight of the sinker and may spit out the hook before the angler has time to set it. Fishfinder rigs, described elsewhere, are therefore favored, particularly when you're after species like channel bass that tend to mouth a bait before trying to swallow it.

Fishing piers come in all shapes and sizes. This public pier at Scusset on the east bank of the Cape Cod Canal in Massachusetts yields species ranging from flounder to bluefish.

As in the case of still fishing, a bait cast off the beach and allowed to soak for some time in one place covers a very little area. If no nibbles have been felt after several minutes, give the reel handle a couple of cranks to move sinker and bait inshore, then wait for several minutes before repeating the process again. You are, to a limited extent, accomplishing what the drifting boat does—covering more bottom and bringing the bait to the fish rather than waiting for it to come to the bait. Work the sinker almost into the wash before casting again, because many species feed where wave action is stirring up sand, gravel, or small stones.

Limited casting is also required when fishing from fixed structures such as bridges and piers, rocky headlands that border a sharp drop-off, and tidal river sod banks. Note that many fishing-pier operators forbid any type of overhand casting because of the dangers to neighboring fishermen. Mastering the flip cast, in which the rod tip is pointed downward, flexed, then snapped forward, pays off. Great distance cannot be achieved, yet it will be enough to clear pilings or other nearby obstructions. Since the line under such circumstances runs almost perpendicular to the water surface—again as with still fishing—rigs with the sinker below the hook or hooks are favored. Several baits at varied depths may be presented simultaneously through the multiple-hook route.

Every bridge or pier casts a shadow on the water below, whether illumination is coming from the sun, moon, or artificial lights. The edge of that shadow line, up-current or down, is prime feeding ground for game species. By casting or lowering baits into that area rather than tossing them indiscriminately, you will get dramatically improved results. Fish tend to lie within the shadowed area with their noses close to the line where the shadow stops.

Bottom fishermen can create their own feeding grounds by chumming—that is, by introducing into the water ground up bait fish, mashed mussels, live grass shrimps, or any other natural food the game species sought prefers. Although such chum may be thrown over the side, whether the side be that of a boat or a shore structure, most of the chum distributed in this manner will float at or near the surface and will not attract bottom feeders until it sinks into the depths far beyond the casting range of the angler. This is especially true when a strong current is running. The trick is to get the chum slick down to the ocean floor.

Bridges are favored platforms for bottom fishermen on all coasts. The trick is to fish the "shadow line."

Chum pots designed for this purpose may be purchased from many tackle shops. The pots are basically weighted, wire-mesh cages. Chum is placed in them and the pot is lowered on a stout line to the desired depth; scraps of bait and oil leach out; and game fish follow the free-lunch line up to its source. Such a chum pot can be made quickly in a home workshop from galvanized or plastic-coated rat wire weighted with lead or stone. An instant substitute is a coarse burlap bag or one of the plastic mesh sacks used for shipping citrus fruit. For small live baits, such as grass shrimps or sand fleas, drop a handful of the critters into a paper bag, add a stone, then lower the whole works to the bottom. When the bag touches down, give the line a sharp yank; the stone will break the bag open so that the chum is released.

Oily baits, such as menhaden or herring, are preferred for most chumming. The oil itself, along with the fish scraps, adds to the attraction. The finer the material is ground, the less chance that fish will gorge themselves before reaching the hook. Although a piece of the chum on that hook will get results, normally it is best to use a bait that is entirely different in character. Thus if ground menhaden is the chum, a sea worm or clam seems to attract more strikes. Perhaps the fish, swimming through a sort of delicious soup, like to gobble down something larger—just as a choosey human will pick a chunk of beef out of a stew.

All sorts of odd materials have been used successfully for chum. A can of cat or dog food is a good example. A piece of line threaded through two holes punched near the top of the can makes a self-anchoring dispenser. Add a few more holes to act as chum-escape hatches. In the Northeast, winter flounder fishermen use canned whole kernel corn or green peas in the same manner. This practice became so widespread that fears were expressed over the possibilities of blocking the digestive tracts of fish which ate the chum but not the hooked bait. Scientists studied the matter and discovered that flounders could swallow products from the Jolly Green Giant without any ill effects. No one determined *why* they were swallowed, since corn and peas cannot be considered common in the marine environment.

Chum made from natural baits can be "stretched" by mixing it with other materials of less value. Regular beach sand will soak up oil, blood, and the general aroma of a ground mix. Uncooked rolled oats also works well, and the fluttering action of each grayish white kernel seems to attract the fish visually. When using mussels, snails, or clams, mash them up with the shells for the scraps of broken shell also have visual appeal.

The best location for chumming is at the edge of a channel, hole, or tide rip where water flows from a comparatively shallow area to a deep one. The fisherman, whether afloat or ashore, should station himself up-current from this edge and allow the chum to be carried down into the deeper water. Baited hook or hooks should be presented slightly down-current from the chum source. As a fish keeps swimming, searching for the master lode of all the goodies, it will run head-on into the angler's offering.

A system of chumming without providing a special supply should also be noted. In shallow water, bottom can be stirred with an oar or pole to release a variety of small marine creatures that will be carried down-current. The same effect can be achieved in deeper spots by bouncing the anchor along the bottom for a few yards before letting it take hold. Even an individual angler can produce a chum line in miniature by lifting the sinker up and down from time to time by rod-tip action. This is recommended primarily when fishing over soft mud or sand: If the sinker is bounced around rocks and ledges, the noise often scares some species away. Underwater sound waves travel much farther than sound waves do through the air.

Sinkers also may be used as visual attractors by coloring them. Yellow is chosen most often with silver a close second. Zinc chromate is the best coating to use for the yellow shade, since it stands up well in salt water. To give a silvery finish dip the lead into a container of aluminum paint. Red serves well in shallow water, but that color appears black to a fish in depths greater than 40 feet.

Luck certainly plays some part in catching fish. However, a consistently lucky fisherman is normally a skilled fisherman who does not hesitate to change his method of attack when the one first tried does not succeed. All the methods described above will take fish, but at times one will take more than the other. It pays to shift tactics when fish are not hitting, just as it pays to shift fishing grounds under the same circumstances.

three

PRIMER FOR

PROSPECTORS

*W*hen we were much younger and thought we knew all about fishing, there were a few jigsaw puzzles that escaped solution. How, for example, did certain old coots of 30 and 40 seem to know precisely where to place hook, bait, and sinker? Even when suffering from that endemic disease of every teen-ager—know-it-all conviction—we thought a form of magic had to be involved. It wasn't luck, for the same anglers always shared the cream of the fishy crop while the rest of us picked up strays.

After a few years of trial and error, understanding glimmered to the surface: It was so simple a thing that it appeared complex! These regulars were "reading the water" long before they buckled-down-Winsocki and delivered bait to a location already decided upon. Fine fishermen spend a fair amount of time prospecting—and perhaps that overworked term, *reading the water,* is a simplification in itself.

First off, one learns to take full advantage of bottom conformation. Inland black bass addicts now call this "structure," and the word is currently moving out to sea. It is a synonym welcomed by crafty old scribblers who dislike reiteration. The ocean angler has a great advantage over his fresh-water brother thanks to the U.S. Government, which provides the nautical chart.

The National Ocean Survey, which is a branch of the National Oceanic and Atmospheric Administration in the U.S. Department of Commerce, publishes charts second to none as far as detail is concerned. They may be purchased at many coastal marine supply stores or from regional offices of the survey. Addresses may be found for the latter in the telephone book under U.S. Department of Commerce in government listings.

These charts give not only shoreline contours and navigational aids, but also depths with holes, shoals, and reefs clearly outlined. Check carefully whether soundings are in fathoms or feet. The latter detailed types are preferred, particularly when you are working sounds and inshore areas. In addition, the character of the bottom is noted, whether sand, mud, rocks, or what have you. Major wrecks are also pinpointed. An angler wise to the ways of his quarry will match the fish to the ocean floor it normally frequents.

If a hot spot is located, mark it on the chart for future reference, and also make a note of what tide phase produces best results. Inshore, cross-bearings on land structures—and the major ones are printed— will give you a navigational fix. Loran coordinates are also part of the chart information, so craft equipped with this navigational gear can return to within a few yards of a good fishing ground. Many party-boat skippers make insurance doubly sure by dropping a marker buoy—a sash weight with a length of line tied to a Clorox bottle suffices—on the spot for future reference.

For those who concentrate on offshore fishing, major tide rips are usually indicated on standard navigational charts, but special ones giving currents, complete with force and direction, are also available from the National Ocean Survey. Coupled with tide and current tables, just about every bit of information there is concerning the fish's watery home is available to the serious angler.

Even without a chart, a good deal may be learned about the structure simply by observing the surrounding land mass. Basically, the ocean floor is a continuation of the coastal shoreline. It just happens to be covered with water. Thus a steep, rocky cliff on the coast of Maine normally extends to deep water and rock bottom close to shore. Shelving sand beaches fronting Cape Hatteras continue in

One aboard and another on the way—once located, fish can provide fast and furious action.

the same manner toward the open ocean.

If the chart does not give you the information on what type bottom it may be, bouncing a sinker over it will give at least some indication of whether it is hard or soft. This is best done by using a handline or simply "feeling" with the line from a reel in hand. The old sounding lead used by coastal pilots had a hollow in its base filled with tallow and this brought up a sample of the ocean floor. Few bottom fishermen are equipped with such gear, but grease smeared on a dipsey sinker will serve much the same purpose. A shell bank in the midst of sand can be located in this manner.

Perhaps because various types of literature over a long period of years have referred to the "ole fishin' hole," neophytes consulting a chart for the first time tend to look for such deep spots as indicated by the soundings in the belief that the hole will be prime fishing grounds. With exceptions we note later, they are not. Seek out what oceanographers call seamounts—underwater hills surrounded by comparatively level bottom. Some of these, like a wreck, are man-made, but the majority have been formed over eons by long-gone glaciers, wear and tear from water currents, years of coastline erosion, busily growing coral, or other natural phenomena. Marine growth establishes itself on such lumps, bait fish follow, and are followed in turn by the predators.

Technology today has produced many fairly low-cost depth recorders, some of which include a print-out paper, illustrating clearly bottom contours. The more sensitive of these will also spot bait schools and individual larger fish. If you have had success over a given seamount, save the graph paper from the machine and write on it the date, time, tidal phase, and fish caught. You will then know just what to look for the next time out.

Lacking a depth finder—and many small boat operators suffer from this lack—pick the brains of commercial fishermen who have been on the grounds before you. Buoys marking lobster and crab pots and fish traps are not bobbing around at random. The fishermen have located payoff bottom and a baited hook dropped in the vicinity has an excellent chance of producing a catch. Ledges, drop-offs, shell banks and the like, which attract creatures crawling along the bottom, also attract those swimming above it. On coasts where there is a large range of tide levels, as on the Northeast Atlantic and Northwest Pacific, commercial operations can also guide inshore anglers to good grounds. Shellfish and sea-worm diggers turn over hundreds of square yards of sand or mud at dead low tide. When the tide covers this plowed ground, fishes gather to feast on the goodies that have been exposed. Drifting over such areas brings rewards.

It is when bottom fishing from the beach, on marl and coral flats, or in tidal creeks and rivers that exceptions to the "hole" rule mentioned above occur. Primarily, the surf fisherman prospects visually. From shore, height of the observer, low tide, and high sun combine to offer the utmost in spotting. With the aid of binoculars and polarized glasses it is possible to determine the exact location of barrier bars and cuts, the latter serving as piscatorial highways to inshore sloughs or surf as the tide builds toward flood. Mussel beds and weed patches appear much darker than surrounding bottom—in fact, we have come to call these "black spots."

Where there is no heavy wave action, areas close to jetties, riprap and similar rock piles often provide fine fishing.

Rock piles or single barnacle-encrusted boulders are easily committed to memory when waters are reasonably clear. Weeds, shell beds, and rubbled ground offer cover for bait, hence predatory game fishes hunt through these sanctuaries and are more likely to hold there or cruise nearby than over clean sand. Here a hole carved by the currents beside a rock may well be the transient home of the game fish sought.

In tidal streams, both large and small, placing bait by the undercut banks will bring much better results than if that same bait is dropped to the bottom in midstream. Note that the holes dug by the river current normally are just *above* a bend. Thus, if you're facing downstream and the river takes a sharp bend to the right, drop the offering close to the bank on the *left* side of the current. That is where deep water, and presumably fish, lie.

Particularly when fishing over inshore flats, the color of the water adds considerable information about its depth and what type of

bottom is likely. Shades range from nearly air-clear to golden translu-
cents, after which they progress to green and blue as depth increases.
In Florida, a depression of no great dimensions may be called a "blue
hole," to distinguish it from close-to-shore channels that are sort of
powder blue. Both are promising locations in which to find a number
of predators that only intermittently prowl the thin water. They
frequent the edges of the drop-offs in order to ambush roving forage
species.

Sometimes it is literally necessary to *feel* one's way. Let's say that you
are hunting corbina on the south California coast. You may be aware
of the fact that they will move shoreward on a flooding tide and may
even be right in the wash at a certain hour. You also know that this
western member of the croaker family practices a musical-chairs
routine, taking advantage of each little pothole out there in the wave-
scoured sand. The trick is to feel out each of these depressions as
sinker and bait are retrieved slowly but steadily. There is here again
that notable change in color—the deeper the water, the darker it will
be in contrast to surrounding ground.

No matter whether you are prospecting from the shoreline or from
aboard a boat, the higher you can get with all due respect to safety
afloat, the better. The platform may be a sand dune, a flying bridge,
or the raised stern of a flats poling skiff: each will give an advantage to
"seeing through" the water surface to spot underwater objects. If eye
level is close to the ocean's surface, even when using polarized sun
glasses, reflected light mars clear vision.

Pier fishermen are already up there. Except when waters are
unusually murky, they can study bottom structure from the beach
edge to the pier's end. Those new to such fishing tend to rush seaward
until they can go no farther in the belief that the deeper the water, the
better the chances of a hook-up. Crafty old-timers stake out a claim
beside some piling farther inshore where they have learned that some
quirk of current on a certain stage of tide draws fish to a point right
under their feet. Such anglers, incidentally, are well worth cultivating
as friends. Many have spent most of their adult lives on or near the
ocean, although they now must confine their fishing efforts to a pier
due to physical infirmity. They often have a wealth of information
tucked away in pleasant memories.

Having prospected and located potentially good grounds, whether in shoal or deep water, normally you should present a bait slightly up-current of the suspected hot spot, then move progressively over the entire expanse down-current. This is done for the simple reason that gamesters usually feed into a tidal flow. While they often will turn to chase quarry that seems to be escaping, it is far more profitable for a predator to hold in one position and wait for bait to come swimming down, borne along and perhaps tumbled by a brisk subsurface current. Although some marine game species may browse along, much like a dairy cow working her way over a clover field, most head against the flow. Therefore bottom feeders for the most part are more active when the tide is not slack.

Beach buggies and surf boats wait out a bad tide at Provincetown, Cape Cod, Massachusetts.

Similarly, where tidal rivers, estuaries, and jettied harbor channels meet the open sea, look for best fishing when the flow is outward. Forage species are carried with the current, often lacking the strength to battle against it. Game fish lie in wait behind a sheltering rock or other obstruction and dart out to take a meal. When the current reverses, you fish on the shoreward side. Experienced bridge fishermen have the timing of such shifts down to a fine point.

Tides are extremely important to bottom fishermen whether jigging in several hundred feet of water or dunking a bait in the shallows. Very few species will remain in one spot throughout a complete tidal cycle. There are exceptions, such as the Atlantic tautog and some of the grouper and snapper families, which, at certain times of year, stake out a claim in some rocky hidey-hole that is well covered with water no matter which way the moon pulls. Even they move with the seasons.

Unfortunately there is no pat rule for determining what is the best tide for all species on all coasts. Surf fishermen have a rule of thumb that the best fishing comes two hours before, and two hours after, slack flood. At the other extreme, in the Annapolis River basin in Nova Scotia a tide bore comes roaring in to float bottom-fishing boats that were high and dry on the flats until the bore reached them. Action is best for a frantic half hour thereafter, then tends to taper off. Experience, or picking the brains of those who have had experience, provides the only true answers.

National Ocean Survey tide tables give times of high and low tides along all coasts of the United States. However, most fishermen depend upon broadcast and print media for this information. Note that the range of tides may have a considerable effect upon success. When there is a neap tide—one in which the rise and fall is at a minimum—fishing is not normally as good as when there is a spring tide, when range is at a maximum. Obviously currents become stronger during the latter period.

Winds can affect tides as well as many other things. In a shallow bay, water may never enter it even on a flooding tide if a strong gale is blowing toward the ocean. Reversed conditions can produce a day when the tide never goes out. When it is necessary to check wind force and direction prior to fishing from shore or boat, consider the fact that wind patterns are predominantly circular with high or low barometric pressure at the circle's center. Therefore, if you live 100 or 150 miles from a favored angling area, it is quite possible that inclement wind direction and force at your home will be precisely reversed on the coast. It is best to call a friend or bait dealer in the area before loading the car and shoving off. And if a coastal full gale is predicted, don't shove off!

Aside from the risk involved, fishing rarely succeeds in stormy weather. In the first place, while certain species are known to engage in feeding sprees just *before* a gale arrives, and just *after* that ill wind disappears, they retire to the depths during the height of the blow and presumably dream of gourmet banquets come calm. In rough seas, anglers find it very difficult to present baits with any measure of finesse: They cannot hold bottom properly; wind bellies every line, and the waves beat a small craft around so severely that hook, bait, and sinker keep jumping as though afflicted with Saint Vitus's dance.

Aside from your ability to locate proper bottom on which certain fish are most likely to be found and to judge proper tides and breezes, there are far more visible indications to guide success. Gulls and terns have been called the marine angler's light cavalry, and that is pretty accurate. On the waterfront, it always pays to be a bird-watcher, for

Great gaggles of gulls and terns usually mean bait is being driven to the surface by game fish below.

these flying spotters rarely get excited unless there is bait to be devoured, or game fish that are moving—working up an appetite.

Swirling aerial circuses of gulls and terns, milling about and often plunging into the swells, invariably mean that forage is available and is being chased topside by predators below. Fury is apparent when game species are slamming into bait on the surface, yet the majority of these ruthless killers are still likely to be hugging bottom. An old salty saw makes the point that when you see a fish on top, there are nine of its fellows below. Note that there may also be more of another species. Thus bluefish tearing surface bait into pieces may well be providing a natural chum slick for fluke close to bottom.

Gulls hovering over a concentration of school stripers close to Virginia's Chesapeake Bay Bridge Tunnel.

Conversely, if all of the various marine birds are resting on the beach, each facing wind direction, it is likely that you are into what is termed a bad tide, especially if you are working the surf. Either sea birds possess remarkable eyesight, or they instinctively know when a feast is scheduled to begin. A tern, apparently flying aimlessly, may suddenly execute a few tight circles close to the surface. One may reason that the graceful creature has seen something interesting. Conclusion: That's a good place to drop a bait down through the lively ripples.

Gulls placidly floating on the surface and craning their astute heads to scan the marine underworld don't do that for fun: They are hunting and figure chances of success are good. Very often bottom feeders—those that lie in wait rather than pursue viciously—flush bait that races toward the sky in order to avoid being eaten alive. Tough on the buffer species—high or low, they are in trouble.

Identification of forage remains of vast importance to a marine angler—and water in which the forage is found means water in which the game fishes are found also. Knowledge of the habits of both are keys to the kingdom. Therefore an angler keeps his eyes peeled both afloat and in the reading room. There are dozens of good identification books on the market: these may not tell you how to present a bait or provide basic training in sea change, yet they detail the habits and types of ground each sea creature prefers. In this connection, A. J. McClane's *Field Guide to Saltwater Fishes of North America* is a good investment.

In addition to keeping eyes peeled, good hearing may play a part in spotting fishing waters, although normally this is useful to those who play the surf or fish the shallows. For example, surfacing snook make a popping noise similar to the explosions of tiny toy balloons. The noise of striped bass chasing bait on top has been compared to that made by running a plastic spoon over an old-fashioned washboard—a musical practice we are willing to bet very few have experienced. Black drum and several of their cousins "boom" even in the deeps—a sound created by expansion and contraction of their air bladders. Tuning in on such fish noises is one more factor that can lead an angler to success.

Another sense which can help a fisherman zero in on his quarry is that of smell. Striped bass exude a sweet, thymelike odor, often even when the fish are not visible near the surface. A bluefish slick smells like fresh-cut melon. Red drum's scent has been described as "musky"—an acrid, almost chemical, aroma. Those who fish for mangrove snappers claim they smell like tanbark. This ability of fish to produce a particular perfume is a mystery. Nobody knows whether it comes from excretion, regurgitation of stomach contents, the mangling of small bait species, or some unexplained glandular phenomenon. It *is* known that these odors are distinctive: night or day, an angler whose nose is well tuned can name his quarry by the fragrance it exudes.

Normally, this scent seems to drift into the air from oily slicks that form on the surface. These indicate fish below, so an immediate presentation of bait is essential before the telltale markers dissipate. Make the offering just up-current from the point where the slick first appeared, not below that point. Count yourself lucky if a multitude of oily patches begins to blossom over a fairly wide area. In that case, although it is never prudent to say *always,* odds shift to favor the on-site angler.

Bottom contours, tides, winds, and currents being equal, time of day must also be considered when seeking out good water. If a high-noon sun is blasting heat down on shallow water, most species swim to deeper and cooler refuges. Follow them and move offshore. That same sun may actually improve fishing in the depths. Bait is driven deeper and within range of predators that haunt the deeps. In a cool overcast, the inshore operator profits.

Bottom fishing at night, except in the case of surf fishermen, cannot be considered standard procedure. However, it is becoming more popular in southern Atlantic and Gulf of Mexico waters and has always been favored along the shores of semitropical islands of both the Atlantic and Pacific. A boat is anchored at the edge of an underwater reef and chum is distributed freely down-current. Snappers and groupers in particular often feed during the hours of darkness and follow the chum line to the baited hook.

Prospecting and reading the water boils down to evaluating each hint gathered prior to and while actually bottom fishing. American Indians used to quip: "White-eyes always *look,* but white-eyes no see!" Maybe that still applies to those of us who carelessly ignore the subtle information that our various seaboards offer 24 hours a day.

four

TOOLS OF THE

TRADE

*E*lsewhere in this book we have said that highly educated bottom fishermen usually acquire a number of different rod-reel combinations, each suited to a specific task and each the most sophisticated, which, unfortunately, may be further defined as the most expensive of its class. True, but while realizing that a few manufacturers may not applaud the following postscript, there is reason to state a case.

One must fly a trainer before graduating to a high performance airplane. Therefore, if you are just muscling into this delightful business of marine angling, ask questions and strive to purchase an outfit that is properly balanced. *Do not immediately invest in the top of the line!*

Likely, in no other book will you read such advice—yet every knowledgeable outdoor writer and sport fisherman will tend to agree. A beginner not only abuses finely honed tools, he finds them handicapping because they are less forgiving than the good standard field grade. There is no onus in starting at the beginning and you can bet your boots that well-made, yet relatively inexpensive, rods and reels are more than adequate.

This is no exhortation to browse cut-rate shelves or dicker with charlatans advertising "complete fishing outfits" for $4.98. Some of the trash coming from foreign countries is not worth the packaging— and be assured that a sorry number of American manufacturers also peddle junk. Whether the product is foreign made or whomped up in the United States, shop for quality. At the outset, how do we define quality?

We don't! Therefore we must go to name brands. Admittedly, such advice may be unfair to fledgling firms turning out remarkably fine equipment, yet there is value in trading with companies that have been in business for many years and have earned the trust of consumers. These outfitters guarantee quality control and they will rarely short-change a buyer. Your new rod or reel may not have an ironclad guarantee clipped to its packaging, but if the item has been marred in manufacture—it happens in the best of families—then the maker will hasten to replace it. Note, in addition, that name-brand tackle manufacturers believe in old-fashioned service and will provide parts on order. Some of the cheapie reels seem to be one of a kind: If a bail spring self-destructs or a gear gets mangled—throw the whole thing into a trash barrel because no replacements will be available.

Not so long ago a rod we were using snapped about midway between ferrule and tiptop. It happened to be a fine field-grade stick made by one of this country's reputable firms, and there had been an obvious flaw in manufacture. So, the matter was duly reported, together with a request for information about the best method of home repair. A new rod arrived by return mail—no charge.

In this case the makers admitted that they were at fault, that a guide-winding machine had unaccountably gone berserk and applied too much pressure to wraps, thus forcing metal seats into hollow fiberglass blanks. Before the fault was noticed and corrected, some of the rods were shipped to wholesalers. No argument, and no sweat concerning replacement. Reputable firms work that way.

Naturally, you get what you pay for and there are hyacinths for the soul in buying the finest of gear. On the other hand, unless there is a crying need for specialization, modern, decently made field-grade rods and reels are only a very small step down from the top-dollar-bracket models. Take, for example, the old Penn Long Beach series of revolving-spool reels. Fin-Nors they are not, yet the Long Beach has gladdened the hearts of millions of bottom fishermen on all coasts for

Matched tackle outfits to fit many needs. Left to right: 50-pound test Dacron line combination for deep jigging; 30-pound test Dacron for medium-depth jigging or still fishing; pier or jetty outfit using 25-pound test monofilament; beefed-up baitcasting rig with 15-pound mono.

many years. They are tremendously effective tools at, relatively, a bargain price. One we bought years ago has been handed down to the third generation as each older owner graduated to a more sophisticated model—and it is still cranking in fish.

A practical bottom fishing outfit need not be expensive, yet it must be well balanced to ensure satisfaction. This terminology is deceiving and is a hangover from the early days of fly fishing when the weight of the reel mounted at the base of the rod butt was supposed to balance exactly with the weight of the forward part of the rod from some arguable fulcrum point. Well balanced now really means well matched.

Do not go to the cut-rate marts of trade all innocence and well heeled. Such bargain shops are best avoided *unless* a shopper knows the true worth of the merchandise offered. Too often the salespeople in these bazaars are not anglers and their recommendations are worthless. Browse cut-rate only after you have acquired the ability to recognize a bargain when you see one. Instead, enlist the aid of a friend who is wise in proper selection, or repair to a shop whose proprietor is a recognized authority. Tell that individual precisely what you intend to fish for and where, then take his advice.

Sport fishing literature devotes much space to ultralight tackle, and we think this is misleading. In the beginning at least, it is far better to invest in standard field-grade gear that is forgiving. Certainly a rod-reel-line combination should not be beefed up to extremes, yet neither should a first-timer try to emulate the featherweight experts of the moment. There will be lots of time later to explore the niceties of sophistication, and fortunately the learning process is a delight in itself. Let's face it: *first, you want to have fun and catch a fish!*

Consider reels as a starting point. The basic choice is between conventional revolving-spool and spinning models. American anglers, who cast to their quarry, cut their sporting teeth in years gone by on the bait-casting outfit and the fly rod. Mastering use of such tackle requires a greater measure of training than is the case with a fixed-spool outfit, since sufficient skill to toss a lure with spinning gear may be obtained in minutes rather than days or weeks. The fly rod holds only a minuscule place overall in bottom fishing, and, therefore, even though we enjoy using such tackle, we pass it by in this discussion. Tossing and retrieving artificial or natural baits with conventional reels requires "educated" thumbs—and some fishermen never acquire a Master's degree in this discipline during the course of a lifetime. In most bottom fishing, casting is not a skill that must be developed to the fine art needed for tournament competition.

Except on relative light-weights such as flounders, surf perches, spots, and a host of other inshore battlers, conventional reels are favored by the majority of skilled bottom-bouncers. Even in the case of the smaller species, spinning reels are used primarily when casting light lures or natural baits in fairly shallow waters. The fixed-spool models are *never* as satisfactory as revolving, when one must present a baited hook or a diamond jig away down in shadowy depths.

Conventional reels are produced in a wide variety of types and sizes. Size designation unfortunately has never become standard among the many manufacturers. Normally the smallest are classified as bait-casting and hold approximately 200 yards of braided or monofilament line. Most of these have a level-wind mechanism geared to move back and forth as the reel handle is turned. This is a notable advantage for those who have not mastered thumb action to level the line smoothly on the retrieve, but friction cuts down casting distance—as noted, not a major handicap for most bottom fishing. However, sand or caked salt in the mechanism will cause frustration. Note particularly that bait-casting models designed purely for fresh water should *never* be used for ocean work. Even with careful rinsing after each trip, they will soon corrode into worthless lumps of metal.

The next types are classified as surf casting reels. They have a wide spool to minimize acceleration of the spool's speed and resulting backlash on the cast. Line capacities vary greatly from about 250 yards to as much as 500. These models are something less than ideal for still fishing or drifting, but are the standard for those working the beaches. For those who have difficulty with thumb control of the spool, models such as the Penn Mag Power and Daiwa Sealine Magforce have been developed with special magnetic devices installed to defeat backlash. Perhaps an educated thumb is being phased out of existence.

Conventional bottom fishing reels normally have a retrieve ratio of $2\frac{1}{2}:1$. Surfmen will have difficulty finding wide-spool specimens less than 3:1, and some are 4:1 or better, to move lures rapidly through the water. Many party-boat anglers now use models with a $3\frac{1}{2}:1$, or better, ratio, not because they want to move their bait or lure rapidly, but because they want to reel in more quickly when the whistle toots to indicate that the craft is moving to another area. Narrow spool reels designed to handle wire or lead-core lines rarely are selected.

The generic term of *bay reel* is used for the next general classification and these overlap with standard trolling reels. These are favorites among bottom fishermen because they are rugged with tough metal spools and good line capacity. Here is where standardization in size numbers among manufacturers would help. The table below gives rough approximations of designated reel sizes and yards of line held.

The line referred to is braided Dacron: for monofilament, add about 10 percent to each.

LINE CAPACITY FOR REELS

Reel Number	30-pound Test	50-pound Test
1/0	230	—
2/0	260	150
3/0	350	200
4/0	450	270
5/0	500	310
6/0	580	400

Even when deep jigging, reels larger than 6/0 are rarely used. The larger models are designed primarily for big-game trolling and are heavy and cumbersome to handle.

Except when using very light gear, metal spools are strongly recommended. Materials include forged anodized aluminum, chrome-plated bronze, and stainless steel. The most rugged are of one-piece construction. Regular plastic spools, especially when using monofilament, can literally explode if much line is retrieved under heavy strain. Mono exhibits a sort of diabolical "memory" when stretched as it shrinks to attain its original diameter. The forces exerted can blow spool flanges apart and rupture side plates as well. We've seen it happen! Note, however, that some firms, such as Carl W. Newell Manufacturing, have developed plastics which can take this punishment—and they are lighter than their metal equivalents.

In both conventional and spinning reels, a good drag is a prime requirement, and a poor one is an invitation to disaster. Perhaps this feature alone distinguishes the quality of the product. A drag that does not operate smoothly is a handicap rather than a help. Often a chattering horror is not caused by poor workmanship at the manufacturing level, but by poor maintenance by the angler. Some seem to feel that slathering of lubricant will cure all ills. Not so! Excessive lubrication may ruin the best of drag mechanisms. Apply it *only* as directed by the maker and do not anoint everything in sight.

Those who feel that we have neglected spinning reels in all the above are perfectly correct. As noted, spinning reels are designed for casting and, in our opinion, should be used for bottom fishing only

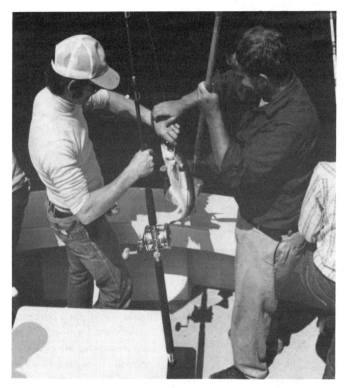

Haddock feed near the bottom, often in deep water, requiring an outfit with plenty of line capacity.

when a light offering is tossed in fairly shallow water or when working the surf. Under the first condition, a quality reel holding about 200 yards of 8-pound test mono is the choice. Although lighter line may be more sporting and may permit longer casts, it can be abraided all too quickly when a bait is resting on the ocean floor. For the surf, match the reel to the quarry and the distance needed to reach it. Dropping below 10-pound test is foolhardy, and most today favor a reel that holds at least 250 yards of 15- or 20-pound mono. Closed-face spin-casting reels tend to gum up almost immediately when used in salt water and are not recommended.

Monofilament line in recent years has become more and more popular for all types of fishing. Although some sing the praises of braided nylon and Dacron for spinning we have yet to be convinced and recommend mono right across the board for fixed-spool outfits. Laboratories for such major mono manufacturers as DuPont, Berkley, and Maxima are gradually making this single-strand extrusion better and less elastic. Sooner or later perhaps we will use little else in all ocean angling; however, that time has yet to arrive.

Increasingly, bottom fishermen are favoring mono on revolving-spool reels for shallow to medium depth presentations—but there is nothing better than braided Dacron where one must offer a bait or lure away down deep. Dacron sinks rapidly and it boasts far less elasticity than monofilament or even nylon braid. It is possible to use single-strand wire on deep grounds, yet it is heavy, springy, and tangle-prone. Another choice is braided wire on medium depth grounds: it is easier to handle on the reel but tends to fray on rubble or rocks. Lead-core nylon braid is another possibility and eliminates the need for very heavy sinkers when the current is swift. Although bulky, it handles well on the reel and does not chew up rod guides as does wire line.

There remains a sometime preference for Dacron braid in heavy surf casting with a conventional outfit; particularly at night a percentage of fishermen find it easier to control than mono. Dacrons today are not "hot on the thumb" as the first ones were, yet we think it better to use single-strand because it tends to resist the surge of wave and current and is less likely to belly in a cross wind. The same characteristics give mono an advantage over braided nylon, which for many years held the top position among those who work the beaches.

No matter what line is used, the reel spool upon which it is wound should be filled to capacity for bottom fishing. This general rule may be modified if the angler concentrates on distance casting from the beach, for then best results may be obtained if the conventional spool is filled to a point slightly below capacity. Overfilling a reel spool will produce line sloughs for the spinning reeler, friction on crossbars for users of the revolving spool.

Backlashes may plague those unfamiliar with conventional reels, not only when casting, but also when simply streaming line to reach bottom from a fixed platform. Correct thumb pressure is the answer of course, but also uneven laying of the line on the retrieve can contribute to the trouble. Instead of staying level, loops flop over one another. In the beginning, we all have trouble laying line correctly. It's not a fine art, but it is an art nonetheless, and it takes a bit of mastering.

Mono, in the hands of a beginning spin-fisherman, tends to twist and become unmanageable. That is not the fault of the line: it is an inherent fault of people who improperly use a spinning reel and crank against an outgoing drag. With each twist of the reel's handle while line is scorching out in the wake of a big fish, you introduce a killing twist. Hold him, pump him, and bring him back—but *never* reel against the drag. The flex of the rod is what eventually renders the fish to possession.

Modern seagoing rods basically are constructed of fibers bonded together with synthetic resins. Terms are deceiving, so an outline of the major types is in order. Solid glass appears solid in cross-section. Here, glass fibers normally are tapered from butt to tip, then bonded in the diameter and length desired. These rods are the least expensive of the various designs, are comparatively heavy for their size, yet are tough and rugged and will take a lot of punishment. Because they are at the bottom of the price range in most manufacturers' catalogs, guides and other fittings tend to be of rather poor quality. The blanks themselves, however, will survive many years of bottom fishing and both guides and windings can be replaced.

Hollow glass, as the name implies, consists of a tapered tube of fiberglass. By varying both the degree of taper and the thickness of the fiberglass wall, almost any desired action can be achieved by the manufacturer. Across the board on all coasts, these are favored by most bottom fishermen since they are versatile, pleasing to the eye, reasonably priced, and may be purchased in a wide variety of weights and lengths. Whereas solid glass sticks require a metal ferrule— usually the link between the butt and the entire tip section—glass-to-glass does the job for the better-grade hollow styles. This means little loss in action even when the rod is broken down into three sections. Note that such ferrules should be twisted while being pushed together in proper alignment. Never try the same technique on metal ferrules for they will part company with the rod material.

Graphite and boron are the latest additions to the rod-makers' stable. Almost pure, or mixed with glass in varying proportions, they add resilience to the blank and improve its casting qualities. Originally expensive, many graphite models now are competitive with high-quality hollow glass, but boron still remains in the top-dollar range. As its use widens, prices undoubtedly will fall. Unless a bottom fishermen wants to have his weapon double in brass as a top-notch casting rod, there is minimal advantage in laying out money for such tackle.

When selecting a rod, make a point of examining guides and fittings very carefully: in almost all cases, they are keystones to quality. Ring guides that have lumpy, rough connections to their frames indicate sloppy workmanship, doomed to part company from each other after minimal use. Reel seats that have no locking ring or similar device will slip under strain to deposit the reel itself at your feet at the most awkward moment. Fancy windings add nothing to strength or action of modern rods as they did in the bygone days of split bamboo; they are just that—fancy windings. If you like them, fine; but do not judge the rod itself by its decorations.

So you now want to select the proper rod, reel, and line combination for the job at hand. As previously noted, a good tackle dealer can be of great help. However, it is obvious even to a rookie that a large and bulky reel mounted on a wispy bait-casting rod *must* be clumsy. By the same token, one instinctively avoids a small and delicate winch paired with a stiff deep-jigging stick. Proper matching of tackle is a skill difficult to describe without writing a veritable encyclopedia listing each rod, reel, and line in popular usage. However, there are some basic categories of combinations which may be cited as properly matched, and a fisherman may interpolate among them when choosing tackle to suit his own particular needs.

Starting at the light end, the seagoing bait-casting outfit consists of a rod with a straight butt rather than the offset handle common to single-handed, fresh-water models. The reel, often level wind, holds at least 200 yards of 10- to 15-pound test monofilament or braid. In the Northeast, such rods normally are six feet overall. Add another half-foot and in the Southeast they are designated as popping rods. Practically the same models, although they may measure seven and a half feet, are termed mooching outfits on the Pacific side. They can handle bait and sinker combinations up to three ounces, but should not be used if the catch has to be cranked through the air up to pier or bridge level. Rod action is too limber to stand the strain.

Built along similar lines are pier and jetty rods, but these have a stiffer action, suited to handle weights up to four ounces, and will survive when reeling a medium-sized catch up to pier level. Most are six and a half to seven feet overall. The matching reel holds about 250 yards of 15- to 25-pound test. Pier rental outfits of this type generally are of solid glass, which will take a good deal of abuse from neophytes.

For offshore fishing in fairly deep water, models classified for trolling are normal. These range from six and a half to eight feet overall with the butt section between 18 to 20 inches. The butt should *not* be fitted with a slotted gimbal nock that fits into a fighting chair. A rubber or plastic cap takes its place and may be snugged into the angler's midsection, with or without a rod belt, when fighting a fish. Action is on the stiff side so that weights of five ounces or more can be handled. Line strength ranges from 30- to 50-pound depending upon the quarry sought. Over 50 is not necessary unless the target happens to be a giant black sea bass or large pot-bellied shark. A minimum of 250 yards of it is good insurance.

For deep jigging, there are two types of outfits in general use. The first consists of a rod six to six and a half feet overall, stiff action, and usually of solid glass. Note that this material should run right through the 18- to 20-inch butt to obtain maximum power and to preclude breakage at the butt-to-tip joint. Reel sizes range from 4/0 to 6/0 filled with 50-pound Dacron. The second option is a cut-down surf blank in the eight-foot range with the same reel-and-line combination. We personally find the eight-footers awkward to handle, but an army of regulars uses them with success. A roller tiptop is a good investment in saving line wear in both outfits.

In the deep waters over the snapper banks on the Gulf of Mexico, electric reels are fairly popular and many party boats there have each fishing station rigged with outlets to accommodate this gear. Unless the fisherman is handicapped by anything ranging from a creaky heart to amputation of an arm, we feel that these devices are primarily meat-fishing tools.

Bottom fishing from the surf line is an entirely different ball game. Here, the trick is to get the bait out to payoff waters. Rod and reel are designed for just that purpose and not as fish-fighting tools. The angler is overgunned for his quarry unless a passing monster happens to inhale the hook. Whether using spinning or conventional reels, overall rod length normally ranges from 10 to 11 feet. Unless you have the height of a basketball player and the strength of a professional wrestler, it is impossible to take full advantage of the power in rods longer than that.

Today, 25- to 30-pound test monofilament is preferred by most surfmen with a shock line nearly double that strength running from a couple of turns around the reel spool out through all the guides, plus several feet of overhang. As noted earlier, fill the spool to near capacity. With a conventional outfit, a half-filled spool will accelerate on the cast as the surface diameter is decreased—and a backlash is almost guaranteed. When spinning, friction of the line on the spool edge increases rapidly as more and more mono heads to sea. This obviously cuts down distance.

Any high surf rod should be able to handle five ounces with ease and still lob even heavier bait-sinker combinations to a satisfactory range. The true long-distance outfits, now popularized in this country by Britisher John Holden's writing and exhibitions of the modified pendulum cast, are powerful and sophisticated. Rather than having the stiff, planky action common to those we cut our surf-casting teeth on, new rods have more power admidships and resilient tip sections. Butts of those in production in the United States are of graphite, although Holden himself has used hardened aluminum in the past. Matching reels are of the best quality—and today's top models are incredibly good.

Distance casting is a skill worth developing for the surfman, not only because there are occasions when one must present a bait away out there, but also because proficiency in long-range heaving ensures greater ease and accuracy at the often shorter killing ranges.

To attain full knowledge about all types of matching tackle may take years for the average angler. The above general guidelines may help lead the newcomer out of the maze that faces him when he examines a rackful of rods in a well-equipped tackle shop. Rather than waggling each of these in a wild manner and thus endangering overhead lights, he should be willing to take advice from those capable of giving it. As the old adage goes, always read the directions—or listen to them.

five

END OF THE LINE

*T*he basic connection between an angler and his catch starts with the hook. Choices in this bit of bent steel are multitudinous. One manufacturer alone, O. Mustad and Son, Inc., of Norway, produces more than 30,000 different types for fishermen all over the world. To select proper pattern and size, it is important to understand not only terminology, but also the function of variations in the hook's components.

Starting with the eye, to which the leader is attached, the styles used in bottom fishing normally are: ringed hooks, which have a round eye lying perpendicular to the bend; turned-up or turned-down eyes, which are offset from the shank at an angle; and needle-eyed hooks, in which a hole is drilled at the leading end of the shank itself. Ringed hooks, usually less expensive than other types, suffice for most bottom fishing. However, if the hook is snelled, a turned-up or turned-down eye insures that the pull will be in direct line with the shank to make presentation of a bait more natural. Specialized needle-eyed hooks are used when threading a delicate bait so that the metal is completely hidden.

Immediately behind the eye comes the shank—the straight part of the hook itself. Short-shanked hooks serve well when small baits such as sand fleas or tiny shrimps are the lure, or when a heavier style may limit the swimming ability of a live bait such as an anchovy. Long-shanked models are preferred when a bait is bulky or has to be threaded along the shank to make a natural presentation. In addition, the long shank will prevent the quarry from swallowing the barb deep in its gullet. If in doubt, stick with the normal shank length that serves a variety of purposes.

Note that in the case of heavier hooks, the lower part of the shank and also the bend often are flattened. Known as forged hooks, these have more strength than those that are simply drawn from round wire. Some other models have the shank sliced or scored to prevent a bait such as a sea worm from sliding down and lumping against the bend. The bend itself may be almost an exact half circle, as in the Aberdeen style, moderately flattened, as is the case with the O'Shaughnessy, or sharply flattened near the point like the Chestertown.

The hook point, which includes the barb, also comes in many shapes and styles. Simplest is the regular rounded wire honed on all surfaces to the point itself. Honing on the inside surface of the barb produces the hollow-point hook, one of the most popular among anglers. The claw or beak point curves well in toward the shank. It is favored by many bait fishermen because the steel tends to make contact with a fish's jaw quickly, and penetrates and holds well. Other hook points, usually in models made of heavy wire, vary from the superior, which is triangular in cross-section, to the knife-edge, which is diamond shaped. Points also may be twisted out of line with the shank—known as kirbed or reversed—designed to hook a fish more readily than a standard model. Their disadvantage is that they cause a bait to spin.

Diameter of the wire from which the hook is drawn must also be taken into consideration. Manufacturers have failed to agree on exact standards, but in general there is light wire, heavy wire, and then sizes indicated by the letter X. Thus an XX heavy or strong hook will be made of wire larger in diameter than an X, an XXX will be even stouter—and so on up to a measure of six Xs.

Selections depend upon three other measurements: point of hook to point of barb; the gap, which is the distance between the shank and

HOOK PARTS

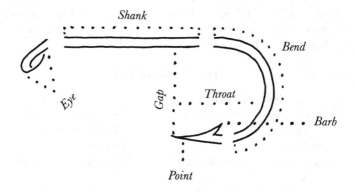

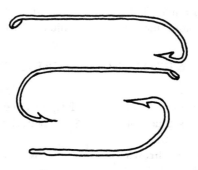

Hook styles (top to bottom):
Aberdeen, Chestertown, O'Shaughnessey

Sliced shank bait hook

hook point; the throat, which is the measurement between the bottom of the bend and a line drawn between shank and point. See the illustration for clarification. If you are now thoroughly confused, take courage! The table below indicates the advantages and disadvantages of these various factors.

HOOK WIRE USED

Small Diameter	*Large Diameter*
Fine point, penetrates easily	Needs more applied force for penetration
Weighs less	Weighs more
Strength sacrificed for size	Strength in proportion to X rating
Springs when it strikes bone	Tends to penetrate bone
Likely to tear tender flesh	Holds in flesh better
Holds small and tender baits	Suitable for more massive baits

POINT TO BARB MEASUREMENT

Short	*Long*
Barb embeds quickly in hard mouths unless it springs	Requires more force for penetration
Hooks may be thrown fairly easily	Once it has penetrated, holds well
Slips out of torn mouth	Holds better in torn mouth

GAP

Large	*Small*
Point extends beyond bait to hook fish	Point likely to be covered by bait
Takes large bite into fish's jaw	Takes smaller bite into jaw
Backs out during long battle	Holds better during battle
Fish may feel hook and spit it out	Hook normally embedded in bait

THROAT

Shallow	*Deep*
Will be covered by small bait	Will accommodate large bait
Shallow penetration, more easily thrown	Deep penetration, holds firmly
Small-mouthed fish hooked readily	Small-mouthed fish may not be hooked

LENGTH OF SHANK

Short	*Long*
Hampers live bait action very little	Retards action of most live baits
Toothed fish apt to cut leader	Protection given against toothed fish
Fish tend to swallow bait and hook	Bait and hook rarely swallowed completely
Fish do not feel metal when mouthing bait	Fish tend to spit out hook when felt
Large baits easily stolen without contacting hook point	Better chance of hooking when using large baits

As is true when selecting any item of tackle, choice of hooks depends to some extent upon personal tastes and habits. However, it is more important to consider the *fish's* tastes and habits. Trying to take a winter flounder with its small, fleshy mouth by means of an **XXX** wire hook with a deep throat is obviously an error. Match the hooks to the jaws they will encounter and take into account what type of battle may follow after the strike. In all cases, keep the hook point sharp. Even new hooks should be honed with a small file or stone to insure maximum penetration.

Hook sizes of course must be considered. In normal bottom fishing, rarely is a hook smaller than number 8 used. In these smaller models, the number designation decreases as the hook shank length increases in steps of one sixteenth of an inch. Thus a number 7 is one sixteenth of an inch longer than a number 8, number 6 the same amount greater than a number 7. For reasons lost in British angling antiquity, when size number 3 is reached, the increments jump to one eighth of an inch. There is no size 0. Instead, sizes go from 1 to 1/0, then to 2/0, and so on up to huge 12/0 tuna hooks. Most manufacturers increase their sizes by half-inch shank lengths after passing size 5/0, yet there are exceptions. It makes little difference: just remember that after they pass the 1/0 classification, hooks get larger as the numbers increase.

Modern salt-water hooks are made of steel or of steel alloy. The bronzed, blued or japanned types common to inland lakes and streams rust away quickly when exposed to the corrosive action of sea water and they should be avoided. It pays to spend a few extra pennies for the best marine hooks available. With an investment by the angler of many dollars in all other tackle, loss of the fish because of a bent or broken hook is stupidity, not economy.

Early stainless-steel hooks were extremely brittle, but, thanks to modern metallurgy, they now meet all angling requirements and do not corrode. Other regular steel hooks are plated. Gold and silver plating reflect light so that the hook itself becomes an attractor, particularly when used with a semitransparent bait, such as a shrimp. However, such plating is thin so, as soon as it wears through and rust attacks the basic steel, throw the damaged item away. Cadmium- and nickel-plated hooks are particularly popular on the Pacific Coast, especially in those smaller sizes used with live bait. They stand up well and, like gold and silver, add a flash to bait or lure. However, the vast majority of salt-water hooks today have a thin cadmium plating overlaid with a heavier one of tin—hence the term *tinned hook*.

Finally, single, double, and treble patterns are numerous. In general, bottom fishermen rarely use double hooks. When selecting a treble for use with a heavy jig or similar lure, check carefully on the quality of the welding or brazing that holds the shanks together. If it is uneven and lumpy, look out! When a fish hits, the treble may suddenly be converted to a double or single as the fish swims away with a sore mouth.

A major terminal tackle item for bottom fishermen is the sinker. With few exceptions, this is made from lead—a heavy, dense metal

SINKERS

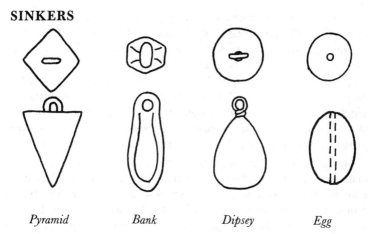

| *Pyramid* | *Bank* | *Dipsey* | *Egg* |

that does not corrode in salt water, is comparatively cheap, and may be cast or molded into a wide variety of shapes and sizes. Despite the many variations, sinkers may be broken down into three major categories: those with sharp edges, like the pyramid, designed to dig into soft or sandy bottom and hold through friction as well as weight; those with comparatively smooth outlines, such as the dipsey, which will minimize fouling on rocks or similar rough ground; those designed to be placed on line or leader, as in the case of split shot or egg-style sinkers.

Weight, of course, is the prime ingredient for any sinker. All other factors being equal, the heavier the sinker, the more quickly it will reach bottom and hold when it gets there. All other factors, however, rarely *are* equal. For example, a pier fisherman using light monofilament line and a wispy rod would be foolish to employ an eight-ounce lead sinker to fish in water perhaps only 15 feet deep. Not only would his tackle be strained to the breaking point, but also he would be unable to detect strikes unless they were violent. Besides tackle, water depth, currents, and the type of bottom must all be considered. A basic rule is to use the lightest possible sinker that will hold the bait in place.

Such lightness has several advantages. First, it puts less strain on line and rod. In addition, as mentioned above, light nibbles will be telegraphed to the rod tip. A sliding sinker or fishfinder rig will help in this department. Once the fish is hooked, a heavy weight cuts down on its ability to give a good account of itself during the fight and also gives leverage against which the quarry may pull to tear the barb free.

As is true of brightly plated hooks, sinkers themselves may be used to attract fish within range of the bait. Yellow, silver, and red, in that order of preference, are finishes which may be added to make the sinker a lure in itself. Although good marine paints may be used to apply color, we opt for nail polish. Believe it or not, some ladies tint their fingertips with yellow as well as red and silver, so almost any color is available at many cosmetic counters. Anglers also may sweeten sinkers with fish oil or by dipping them into a chum bucket.

If the bottom is unusually foul so that sinkers are lost regularly, a small cloth bag filled with sand or pebbles may be substituted for lead. A bit of chum added to the mix serves as an attractor. The bag is connected with line or leader by a bit of light thread which will break under comparatively light pressure. Hook and bait may then be recovered without damage. In roll-your-own country, a Bull Durham tobacco sack is ideal for this purpose.

In addition to sinkers and hooks, leaders are often an integral part of terminal tackle used by bottom fishermen, even though, in this age when monofilament line is used widely, many anglers dispense with such a connection in certain types of fishing. Leaders serve a definite purpose, however, one of which is to reduce chances of a toothed fish biting its way to freedom or rubbing the material connected to the hook against coral, barnacles, or rocks and thus avoiding capture.

Stainless-steel wire is a basic non-biteable material and it is classified by gauge number. Number 2 is .011 inch in diameter with a breaking strength of approximately 27 pounds. This wire runs up to number 16, which is .037 inch in diameter and breaks at 322 pounds. Unless the angler is a shark specialist, number 10 with a breaking strength of 120 pounds is the heaviest needed for most practical fishing. If the water is exceptionally clear, nonreflecting wire is recommended so that the fish is not spooked by the flash of regular stainless.

Wire, because of its stiffness, has the advantage of holding the hook well clear of sinker and line. This very advantage, however, is also a handicap. If the wire becomes bent or kinked, it is almost impossible to straighten it out again to its original form. If the kink is sharp, even number 10 wire will break under a few pounds of strain. Cable wire overcomes the kinking problem to a large degree, yet it cannot be twisted easily onto a hook or swivel as is the case with single-strand stainless. Sleeves and a crimping tool provide the answer, yet we lean toward another solution—nylon-covered cable. This material, in strengths below 50 pounds, may be knotted in much the same manner as monofilament nylon. The knot need not be elaborate with a simple figure eight sufficient to do the job. Actually more bulky knots, such as the improved clinch, will give the leader a permanent crimp just above the hook where it is least wanted.

Nylon itself is standard leader material for many bottom fish which do not have teeth sharp enough to cut through it. As mentioned above, many anglers seeking the smaller species connect sinker and hook directly to a monofilament line. Abrasion can be a problem when this is done and any knot weakens the line to some degree; therefore a leader about 50 percent stronger than the line itself is good insurance against breaks.

In heavy surf casting, because of tremendous pressure exerted when a rod is fully loaded to attain maximum range with baited hook and sinker, the so-called shock leader or shocker is much used. This trace serves two purposes: It permits the use of far lighter running line than what used to be considered standard—the light line ensures greater range than the heavy—and it also performs as does a standard short leader to prevent cutting off by sharp-toothed fishes and possible terminal abrasion.

A shock leader is always long enough to permit practical overhang from a tiptop, and then to proceed back through the guides and make several turns around a reel spool. Strength largely depends upon rod power and the amount of stress generated in casting. Fifty-pound test nylon will suffice with the gutsiest of conventional high surf sticks, and one can scale down to 30 or 40 with the average surf spinning outfit. Here, the first and most important requirement is insurance against break-off at the moment of maximum rod loading prior to release.

Although leaders, hooks, and sinkers may be tied directly to the line, somewhere in the connecting process snaps and swivels are normally a part of terminal tackle. The combinations and varied uses of these are described in detail in the chapter about rigs, but a word on the hardware itself is in order. The most important rule is to use as few snaps, swivels, and other connectors as possible. Excess weight that

SWIVELS

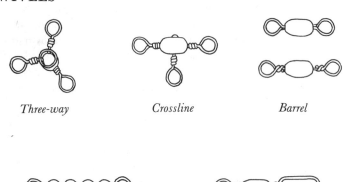

Three-way   *Crossline*   *Barrel*

Bead chain   *Lockfast*

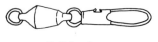

Ball bearing

kills the natural action of bait or lure, high visibility that spooks the fish, and edges that tend to snag or to collect weeds and grasses, all are factors favoring a minimum.

As in the case with hooks, swivel sizes range from small, number 12, through number 1, 1/0, 2/0, and so on. Standards vary among individual manufacturers, but they are close enough for purposes of comparison. Often the swivel used will be of far greater strength than the line or leader to which it is very shoddily made. Pay a little extra and get the best.

Note that even the best swivels are not 100 percent effective in preventing line twist when a lure or bait spins frantically. Use of a keel or keel sinker will help cure this trouble. To keep swivels functioning at maximum efficiency, rinse them in fresh water after prolonged use and give them a squirt of water-displacing lubricant such as CRC or WD-40 to aid in battling gumminess or corrosion.

A single swivel is a standard connection between line and leader.

Use the smallest size that will accommodate the diameter of these two items. The three-way swivel is a favorite among bottom fishermen because the line may be attached to one ring, the sinker to another, and a snelled hook to the third. The cross-line is a variation of this and provides a straight pull between the two end-swivel rings—an advantage when trolling, but of marginal value when bottom fishing.

Concerning snaps, the original safety-pin style is still used to some extent in fresh-water fishing. Under strain, it tends to fly open and also it will corrode rapidly in the briny. In recent years, a wide variety of stainless-steel locking snaps have been developed and all are far more efficient than the safety pin. They range from the Duolock, twisted from wire, to the McMahon, which is designed on the principle of ice tongs. Choice depends upon the need to cut down bulk, strength desired, and personal preference, with this last condition undoubtedly the most important.

So much for the basic items of terminal tackle. There are dozens of others which will be covered in the discussion on rigs that follows.

SNAPS

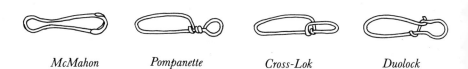

McMahon   *Pompanette*   *Cross-Lok*   *Duolock*

Lock Snap   *Safety Pin*   *Sinker Snap*

six

KEEP IT SIMPLE

*P*owers of invention and imagination rank high among the qualities of a good fisherman. Big-game buffs may toy with kites,
outriggers, and even underwater strobe lights to outwit their quarry.
Casters take pride in altering a perfectly good factory-made lure to
enhance its action or color. Trollers devise all sorts of space-age
schemes to get a hook into a fish's mouth. With bottom fishermen,
this tendency finds an outlet in rigs—combinations of hooks, sinkers,
swivels, and other hardware that may produce better results than
what are commonly used.

In such developments, we follow the KISS school: "Keep It
Simple, Stupid." However, circumstances often arise when a basic rig
just does not catch as many fish as one that is more complicated. Start
with the basics, then elaborate as the spirit—and the fish—moves.

One basic rig involves a three-way swivel, sinker, and snelled hook,
or a leader and hook. Line is tied to one eye of the swivel, the sinker to
the second by means of a short length of line, and the hook to the
third. Simple enough, yet there are several factors to consider.
Keeping the sinker attachment short obviously will result in the baited

hook resting right on the bottom with a minimum chance of the components fouling each other. Chances of such fouling are increased in almost direct proportion to the length of this connection.

If the fish sought normally feeds just above the ocean floor, a longer sinker line allows presentation of the bait at slightly higher level while still holding fast to bottom. By keeping tension on the line—not sufficient to lift the sinker clear—you can keep the hook free of obstructions. A second hook may be used, but this increases tangling problems by a factor of about 100 percent. The three-way swivel rig is satisfactory for both still fishing and drifting. In the latter case, length of snell or leader should be increased to eight inches, or even eight feet with a live eel, so that the baited hook will trail well behind the sinker. Mud, sand, and the like stirred up by the lead serve as a miniature chum line, and the longer leader insures that the hook rides in this attracting cloud.

If the line is kept taught, even a light strike will be telegraphed to the rod tip. However, the fish may feel the drag of the sinker on the bait and abandon efforts to dislodge it. The fishfinder was developed specifically to overcome this problem. There are many types, ranging from a simple snap swivel to a center-drilled egg sinker. All function in the same manner. Line is threaded through the eye of the fishfinder, then tied to a swivel at the end of the leader with that swivel large enough to check passage. The sinker is then added to the bottom-linking mechanism. When a fish hits, the rod tip is dropped slightly and species like channel bass, which mouth a bait before moving it back to crushing teeth, will not feel any weight or become alarmed. Strike when the fish really starts to move.

Although the fishfinder was originally developed for use in the surf, it may be adapted successfully to almost any type of bottom fishing. When sinkers weighing four ounces or more are rigged ahead of baited hooks, nibbles that might be undetected with a three-way swivel rig will be felt, whether the platform be beach, bridge, pier, or boat deck.

Note well that sinkers are *not* always rigged ahead of a baited hook. In most inshore bottom fishing, they are below the hook, which gives rise to countless arrangements of terminal tackle. In general—and there are many exceptions—species that feed in deep water at or near the bottom appear to prefer a potential meal that swings clear *below* a sinker, whether that sinker is resting on the ocean floor or is being

FISHFINDER RIGS

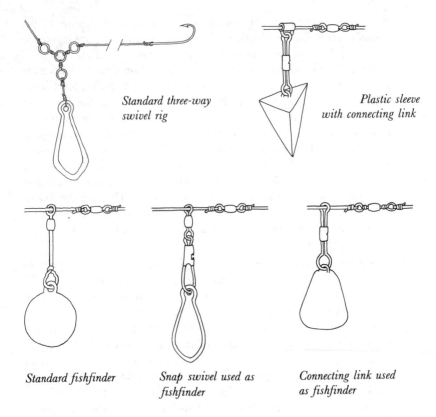

Standard three-way
swivel rig

Plastic sleeve
with connecting link

Standard fishfinder

Snap swivel used as
fishfinder

Connecting link used
as fishfinder

fished at mid-depth. Experimenting with Atlantic cod in waters about 10 fathoms deep, we found that the old kidney-shaped sinker trailing an 18-inch leader and clam-baited hook—the rig used by handliners on the Grand Banks more than 100 years ago—outfished a dipsey sinker of the same weight that was hugging bottom with the leader attached a foot above it with the same bait, at a ratio of at least 2:1. Don't ask us why!

Two hooks may be rigged below a sinker, one with a short snell and the other with a long. More than two will cause tangling trouble. Although these two hooks may be tied in tandem, one behind the other, we prefer to have separate snells for each and each attached to the sinker itself. An advantage of this system is that if a fish is hooked, chances are good that another may take the second bait while it is dragged through the water during the fight. If hooks are rigged in

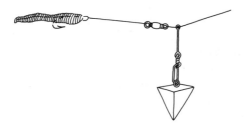

Fishfinder with seaworm

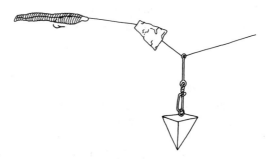

Fishfinder with cork added to keep bait clear of crabs

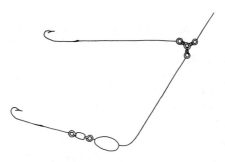

Three-way swivel and sliding sinker, used primarily when drifting

tandem, the fish's body may intervene to make a chance at a double unlikely.

Inshore on all coasts, the drop sinker with hook or hooks rigged *above* it normally is more successful than the deep-water combination. The basic outfit consists of a sinker tied to the end of the line, then a snelled hook attached above it by means of a simple loop knot in the line itself. Swivels, with the cross-link three-way model preferred, may be used for this purpose, but we avoid excess hardware whenever possible. Many choose what originally were termed "buttons" now also termed *quick rigs*—bits of colored plastic tubing about an inch long drilled to one-eighth inch with grooves at each end to hold line and snell loop. Doubled line is thrust through the tubing, the snell loop is then linked to this and the whole rig snugged up tightly. Buttons do away with the need of tying loops in the line itself, thus weakening it, and their color may be an added attractor for the fish. Although these are available in some tackle shops, many anglers make their own by cutting up plastic tubing of suitable diameter and smoothing any rough surfaces with emery cloth.

Probably the best known of all rigs using a sinker with hooks rigged above it is the high-low type, usually written hi-lo. Here one hook is tied into the line just above the sinker and another, at least a foot above it. This presents baits at two different depths for fish moving right along the bottom and those slightly above it. Some start out with three or more hooks rigged in this manner, then if fish are taken on a regular basis at one particular level, the other hooks are removed.

Variations on the hi-lo rig are legion. Often the hook sizes will vary when on grounds where two or more species may be taken. One type of bait may be used on the lower hook with another on the high one. For example a Pacific angler might bait his bottom 2/0 hook with a chunk of herring for lingcod and a tiny number 6 decorated with a bit of lugworm would ride higher to entice a wandering rockfish. It is best to have the larger hook and bait lower on the terminal tackle totem pole whenever possible to minimize tangling.

A specialized hi-lo rig sporting half a dozen or more hooks may be used when after bait fish or species such as mackerel, which tend to travel in dense schools. Although natural bait may be used, normally small spoons or short lengths of plastic tubing are the lures. The whole rig is lowered to whatever level is desired, then jigged up and down. Multiple hook-ups are the rule—hardly the most sporting method of

Standard Hi-Lo rig

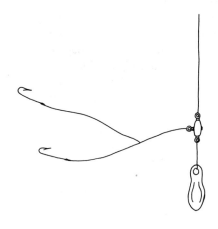

Twin hook rig

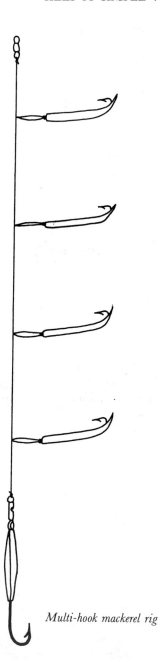

Multi-hook mackerel rig

STANDOFFS

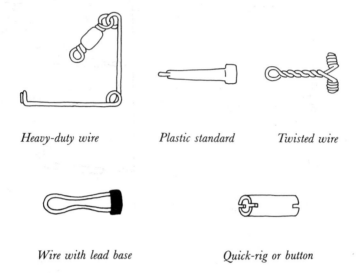

Heavy-duty wire   *Plastic standard*   *Twisted wire*

Wire with lead base   *Quick-rig or button*

fishing, yet useful when a bait well needs filling.

In addition to knotted line loops and the buttons mentioned above, several other devices have been developed to keep the hook clear when a line is running almost perpendicular to the bottom. These may be made of wire or plastic and they vary widely in design. Many are available in package rigs already made up by the manufacturer. Avoid the cheaply priced items that tend to include shoddy materials. Our objection to many of these, even in the better quality lines, is that they include too much unnecessary hardware.

The term *standoff* is used in some areas to describe such components, but the average tackle shop operator will look bewildered if you ask for it under that name. He will look even more bewildered if you mention the British term *lear* and might refer you to Shakespeare's unhappy king or to the nearest private jet airport. Call them "those things that look like a half-spreader" and salesmen seem to understand. Select the lightest possible to match the fish you seek.

Spreader rigs themselves are favorites in many areas, particularly when the quarry is comparatively small, such as winter flounder or spot. Prone to tangle, such rigs should be lowered into the water rather than cast. Line is attached to a swivel at the midpoint of the

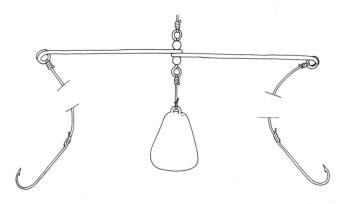

Standard flounder spreader rig

wire arm with a sinker tied in below it. Snelled hooks are then attached to the rings provided at each end of the wire. As the name implies, spreaders are designed to keep two baits apart and thus to cover a wide area on the ocean floor. To minimize tangling, have the whole rig perfectly balanced with an equal weight of bait on each hook. Also have the hook snells short enough so that they cannot foul each other. Doubles are common when fishing with spreaders, so if one fish has been hooked, pause a moment before reeling in and another may take the remaining bait.

Some less cautious than we are will put two snelled hooks on each spreader eye or will use a double spreader, with the two arms rigged at right angles to one another. This may enlarge the area covered and offer more bait to fish in the vicinity. However, such combinations are awkward to handle and are lethal to hands and fingers when the catch is swung into the air. Flapping fish and flying hooks can cause much trouble to the human epidermis.

Far removed from spreaders, but useful in much bottom fishing, are floats. The word conjures up the picture of a farm boy equipped with cane pole, short line, bent pin, and can of earthworms. No modern farm boy in his right mind would use a bent pin, yet the

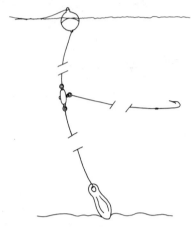

Float and sinker rig

stereotyped image favored by calendar publishers is hard to dispel. In marine bottom fishing, floats are used in two ways. First, the standard presentation with the float bobbing on the surface with sinker and baited hook below it; the second and much more common is a float of some sort mounted between the hook and the sinker itself.

In the first category, a plastic bobber or cork can be used to advantage when trying to cover difficult areas. For example, when fishing from a bridge under which a strong current is flowing, streaming a great deal of line with sinker and baited hook at its end will result in a large slack loop that will be buffeted by the currents in a dozen different ways. If a fish hits, it is difficult to drive the barb home because of this slack. Particularly in shallow water, use of a float under such conditions will enforce a comparatively straight connection to the rod tip with most of the line either clear of the surface or right on it. Sinker weight should be sufficient to get the bait down to payoff grounds, yet not heavy enough to drag the float under. Experimentation will determine the length of line required between float and sinker to reach the fish.

If the current is so strong that sinker weight needed to hold bottom drags the float under the surface, use a drop-sinker rig with the hook or hooks above it. The sinker may be cast or worked down-current to the spot desired, and the float is then positioned almost directly above it as shown in the sketch. When the bobber disappears, brace your feet! This same system works when boat fishing or when working the sod-bank edges of a tidal stream.

Floats themselves can be attractors—hookless lures of a sort. The classic example of this type of rig has been used for many years in the Southeast, both on the Atlantic and Gulf sides, by seatrout anglers. Shrimp is the favored bait with a split shot or small clamp-on sinker fastened a foot or two above it. The leader is monofilament and line may be of the same material or of Dacron.

A cork float, which gurgles and pops when the rod tip is twitched, is rigged so that it rides on the surface. Water depth of course determines the distance from cork to hook. Seatrout come to see what the disturbance is all about then latch onto the trailing shrimp. This rig may be adapted to almost any species that feeds in the shallows.

Floats mounted between hook and sinker are used to keep the bait off bottom out of handy reach of crabs and other scavengers. Used with any rig from fishfinder to drop sinker, they also give added action to either live or dead baits. In the days before medicines were bottled with tamper-proof caps to frustrate both children and adults from gaining access to the contents, the inch-long corks then used were ideal for this type of rig. Sliced halfway through lengthwise, they could be slid onto leader or snell and would hold fast in whatever position desired. Such corks are still available from friendly pharmacists and are a good addition to any tackle box.

The float itself may be part of the lure, such as in the case of the Jersey Doodlebug, mentioned in the chapter on methods of fishing, or the fluorescent Fireball, popular along the coasts of Virginia and the Carolinas. Be warned when using such rigs: do not have the float so large that it tries to surface, carrying the hooked bait up to foul on line or leader. Buoyancy should be almost neutral so that the combination works in the current clear of the bottom, yet also clear of the line.

On the opposite side of the coin, negative buoyancy may be provided by split shot or small clamp-on sinkers when a bottom fisherman employs the technique known as live-lining. True live-lining is done by streaming a bait slowly down-current, then retrieving it in foot-long stages, only to be streamed again. A good deal of water may be covered by this method, but obviously bait and hook will ride high at or near the surface. Adding the light sinker a foot or more ahead of the bait will bring it within feeding range of bottom feeders. This system is particularly effective when currents are gentle.

Split shot, clamp-on sinkers, strip lead, and lead wire are all useful when making up bottom rigs. We favor the first two named because, once crimped in place, they do not slide along line or leader. The combinations are many when utilizing these light weights. For example, in a three-hook hi-lo rig, a small cork may be placed on the top hook, no weight or float on the middle one, and a split shot on a fairly long snell or leader at the bottom. The three baits will then cover water levels vertically from the bottom itself up to several feet from bottom. Keep the top snells fairly short—not more than 10 inches—to minimize tangling. In addition, crimp the sinker on the lowest rig just in front of the hook eye. Although this cuts down on bait action in the current, it will also cut down on self-tangling.

Many anglers add colored beads and other decorations in a similar manner to provide weight as well as to serve as attractors. Used in moderation beads may be of help in making a bait more enticing, but we have yet to be convinced that festoons of them covering several inches of snell or leader serve a useful purpose. This may well be because of our general KISS philosophy when bottom fishing.

As noted elsewhere, we do not favor extensive use of other attractors like flashers and spinners for most bottom fishing. However, when drifting for species such as the toothed flounders, one or two spinner blades rigged between sinker and hook increase catches to a marked degree. For best results, have the spinner a minimum of six inches ahead of the hook's eye. A strip bait of squid or fish belly completes the ideal combination with this rig.

Every coastal area has its own special rig for special species. Each season new combinations are developed which, at least for a short time, seem to take more fish than the old-time standards. Local tackle shops and anglers can provide up-to-date information. Follow their directions and, if you get no results, try something different! Such experimentation separates the skilled angler from those who are classified as unlucky.

seven

BAITS UNLIMITED!

*F*ish have to eat in order to survive. Bottom fishermen depend upon this fact for success and, in the majority of cases, use natural bait in which a hook has been embedded as the basic lure to tempt their quarry. Choices are legion and vary from bits of vegetable matter eaten by some of the Pacific surf perches to whole live fiddler crabs rigged to catch tautog or blackfish of the Northeast.

Although coastal tackle and bait shops sell a wide variety of such natural baits, many anglers prefer to catch, net, or dig their own. At the outset, therefore, we post a warning: regulations on taking of bait, whether it be a clam or an anchovy, are many and often very local in application. *Before* using a minnow seine at the edge of a tidal river or wielding a clam hoe on a mud flat, check not only state regulations, but also rules set forth by coastal townships concerning such harvesting. Penalties for violations may be severe—and being booked by a warden before the fishing trip has even started is a poor plan of operation. Remember that ignorance of the law is no excuse when standing on the wrong side of the judicial bench.

Regulations regarding clam digging come high on the list of laws concerning taking of natural bait, for these bivalves are popular as human food. The soft-shell, known also as steamer and man-nose, is a favorite among anglers where the species is commonly found. In the East, soft-shells dig in mud and sand flats from the edge of the Arctic to the shores of North Carolina and have been introduced successfully into waters of northern Florida. Their burrow holes often may be seen at low tide and a small jet of water will squirt skyward if they are disturbed. In the Pacific, they have become established in some areas from southern British Columbia to mid-California, but not in the quantities common to their native Atlantic grounds.

Shucked clams of this species have a rather tough neck or siphon, which will stay on a hook firmly. The belly, gills, and other internal workings are soft and make a prime bait for bottom feeders. The best way to hook this critter whole is to pierce the round belly through, twist connecting tissue between belly and siphon a couple of times, then impale the siphon lengthwise so that hook barb and point are exposed. The soft parts of the clam will then be well up on the shank and will not be nibbled away as easily as when at the point.

When after such species as tautog, which are equipped with shell-cutting teeth, do not shuck small clams at all. Crack them slightly between two rocks and drive the hook point completely through both shells and meat. Small pieces of the soft-shell may also be used to take fish ranging from smelts to flounders. Peel the black "skin" from the neck for best results. Some anglers feel that dipping clams into red vegetable dye improves their catching powers—a scheme we have never tested thoroughly.

There are many species of hard-shell clams, more circular in shape than the soft-shell, but they are used more for human food than for bait since they are soft-bodied and difficult to thread on a hook. Found buried in sand or mud of tidal waters from Canada to Florida and in much of the Gulf of Mexico, the smaller sizes are known to restaurateurs as cherrystones and littlenecks while full-grown adults are quahogs to New Englanders. We mention these clams not because they are a preferred bait, but because they are often available when other bivalves are scarce—and they take a wide variety of bottom feeders.

As is true in the case of other soft baits, winding a light thread or narrow rubber band around hook shank and meat will help prevent soaking off. However, we have never found this practice particularly

Soft clams, often called steamers, make good baits. A plumber's helper can suction-pump clams out of sandy flats, but on a mud bottom it is less effective.

efficient when clams or mussels are involved. Use of water-soluble plastic wrapping is an alternative that shows promise.

Largest of the Atlantic clams normally used for bait is the surf, ocean, or skimmer species. As the first two names indicate, these are found in deeper water than their soft-shell look-alikes; they grow to a length of more than seven inches and make a tough tempter, either whole or cut in pieces. Their range is from the northern Atlantic through North Carolina. A slightly smaller cousin is found from Cape Hatteras to Florida.

During a heavy storm, particularly in the area from southern New England to the Delaware line, vast numbers of skimmers may be torn from their beds and tossed up on coastal beaches. Fish of all shapes and sizes, plus many sea birds, will feast on this natural chum line day and night. Under these conditions, even a surf clam that has been exposed to sunlight and air so that it has an overpowering aroma can be an effective bait. This is one of the exceptions to the general rule that fresh bait takes fresh fish.

The Pismo clam of the Pacific, which ranges from the beaches off San Francisco into northern Mexico, is an equivalent to the skimmer but is valued far higher as gourmet food for humans. Laws concerning its harvesting therefore are strict, and it is unlikely that many of the succulent bivalves now serve as fish bait. When Pismos were abundant years ago, they were widely used to tempt species ranging from surf perch and corbina to a number of others. Undoubtedly anglers still use a few for this purpose. As with the surf clam, because of its size, pieces of meat (rather than the entire body) are threaded on a hook. Tailor each chunk to suit the size of the quarry's mouth—tiny bits for surf perch and larger gobs for corbina.

Many other species of clams are found on all coasts, but are not commonly used as bait due to lack of availability in quantity. A possible exception is the jackknife or California razor clam—a bivalve with a long and narrow shell and one used as a favorite food for croakers. Harvested primarily by noncommercial diggers along the Southern California coast, it boasts fairly firm meat which may be used whole or in pieces. Atlantic razor clams may also be used as bait but are seldom thus employed.

Mussels are found on all coasts, clinging to rocks, pilings, and underwater obstructions near the tide line. Their meat is extremely soft and difficult to keep on a hook. Crack the shells of smaller specimens and use them shell and all for bait. By parboiling larger mussels for about two minutes in salt water, you can toughen the meat enough to prevent almost immediate soaking off the hook. Crushed mussels make an excellent chum, which may be dribbled over the side of a boat or shore structure in shallow water. A chum pot or weighted mesh bag will do the trick when water is deep. Note that crushed shells of any clam or mussel, even after meat has been removed, can serve as chum. The small bits of flavored shell fluttering down through the water have both taste and eye appeal.

Shellfish of any kind may be kept for several days if bedded in seaweed and stored in a dark, cool spot. *Never* moisten them with fresh water, for results will be fatal to the bivalves. If prolonged storage is desired, immerse the baits in a covered wire-mesh basket or slatted wooden box in salt water where currents will keep both air and water circulating. Pick a shady spot so that sunlight will not raise the temperature to a killing point. A bucket of sea water is a poor compromise, because oxygen is soon depleted and the water itself tends to heat up.

Almost every youngster who starts fishing in coastal waters is initiated to another form of shelled bait which is plentiful below high-tide mark and is easily gathered at no cost with little effort. Snails and periwinkles abound and come in assorted shapes and sizes to the delight of conchologists. Fishermen pay little attention to the distinctions among species, but the moon snails of both the Atlantic and Pacific are preferred basically because they are larger than their periwinkle cousins. When the shells are cracked open, the extracted meat is tough and several snail bodies may be impaled on a hook to attract many of the smaller bottom feeders. These mollusks make a fine emergency bait source.

Whelks and conchs, with some of the latter weighing up to five pounds, are the giants of the snail clan. Their meat makes an extremely tough bait, which may be softened by pounding it with a wooden mallet. Strips or chunks, cut to suit the size of the fish sought, work well enough but may be made more enticing by adding a bit of some softer bait such as a clam to the hook. In days gone by, the whelk was a traditional bait in North Atlantic waters for cod and haddock, but, because catching it in quantity is time-consuming and involves a trap holding dead fish set in fairly deep water, it has fallen from favor. Conch, on the other hand, remains popular in tropical and semitropical areas for species ranging from bonefish to groupers.

Although classified as a mollusk by scientists, to a layman squids have very little resemblance to clams and snails. There are many species of these jet-propelled sea creatures and they are found on all coasts. Voracious, they will feed on fish and even on each other. In some areas, anglers make a sport of jigging for squid, primarily at night under artificial light, with a lead weight into which has been

Baits often used for red drum (channel bass). Top to bottom: spot, squid, crab, and cut spot ·

molded a ring of barbless, sharp spines. Squid jigs may be improvised by sliding an egg sinker or plastic tube over a treble hook from which the barbs have been removed. When a squid is hooked, do not swing it immediately within grabbing distance because it squirts a shot of "ink" as a defense mechanism. Most fishermen are content to buy squid, either fresh or frozen, from bait shops or food stores, where it may be sold under the Italian name of *calamari*. Sometimes schools of squid will be driven ashore by game fish, and an angler may replenish his supply easily.

Squid, either whole or cut in strips, makes an excellent bait for species ranging from swordfish to sea bass. The meat is tough and will withstand onslaughts from many nibblers, such as crabs and cunners. The head, with the hook passed through the eyes, has particular appeal to striped and channel bass and to large weakfish. Squid strips make an excellent addition to artificial lures when bouncing these off the bottom. Both scent and wriggling action attract predators.

If the bait is to be kept for any length of time, it is wise to remove the entrails, then store the body of the squid in a cooler or freeze it. Salt will help in the preservation process, but it toughens the meat unduly and induces a color best described as shocking pink. Sunlight and heat cause the flesh to rot quickly—and a spoiled squid, which also turns pink in color, produces an odor that will make your eyes smart!

Completely different from squid both in appearance and scientific classification are the sea worms. There are many species, most of which burrow in sand, gravel, or mud for much of their lives, but the two major groups used for bait are those of the genus *Nereis* and the genus *Glycera*. Species of the former are known as sand worms or clam worms along the East Coast and pile worms, rock worms, or mussel worms in the Pacific area. *Glycera* are commonly called bloodworms and, although there are small populations of several species in Pacific waters, their greatest abundance is from the Canadian Maritime Provinces to the Carolinas on the Atlantic side.

Clam worms as a group have rounded backs, flat bellies, distinct segments along their bodies, and a series of leg-like appendages along each side. The head is equipped with a stout pair of nipping jaws. Color varies from greenish blue to reddish brown depending upon the environment and upon the particular species. Bloodworms are softer and more easily torn apart than clam worms and, when broken, exude a liquid the color of human blood. They are cylindrical in shape, lack the "legs" found on the *Nereis* tribe, and have four hook-like jaws rather than two. In color, they are more pink and red than clam worms.

There is a brisk trade in sea worms throughout the fishing season. The major tidal areas, from which they are dug in much the same manner as clams, are located in the Canadian Maritimes and north-

Seaworm, also called a clam worm, showing nippers at the head.

ern New England. Packed in cartons—called flats in the trade—that are filled with rockweed as bedding, they are air-shipped to all coasts for retail sale. A flat normally contains a gross of worms and bait dealers break these down into small boxes to be sold by the dozen. Many anglers insist upon selecting their own choice of worms from the flat and show as much care in this operation as an inland trout fisherman does when choosing a dry fly.

Sea worms may be kept for a couple of weeks if allowed maneuvering room in a bed of rockweed or sea lettuce moistened regularly with salt water. Fresh water will kill the worms almost instantly—and one dead worm causes the death of others quickly. A container, allowing free circulation of air, should be kept darkened and, if possible, under refrigeration. It is advisable to invert the container or shake up the contents daily to prevent sea worms from matting together. Note that bloodworms and clam worms should not be stored together, for they will attack each other. Although breeding of sea worms in captivity has been done successfully on an experimental basis, it has never been accomplished to date on a commercial scale.

As noted in chapter 2, threading a sea worm along the hook shank

Worms properly bedded in seaweed moistened with salt water. They will die almost immediately if any fresh water is added to the bedding.

Seaworm hooked at the head so the squirmer will stream naturally.

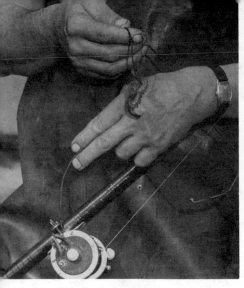

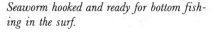
Seaworm hooked and ready for bottom fish-
ing in the surf.

Use this method to hook hard-shelled crab.
Soft-shells can be secured to the hook with
rubber bands or fine thread windings.

so that its tail streams out beyond the hook bend is an efficient way of presenting such baits. Special "worm hooks" with a small, needle-sharp point wrapped in to protrude just above the eye are still available in some coastal tackle shops. When the head of the worm is impaled on this pin, the squirmer will not slide down the shank and bunch up on the bend. Today's fishermen more often employ the sliced-shank "bait-saver" hook, which does the job just as well (and will also shred the finger bones of a careless angler who thoughtlessly strips a shopworn worm off between compressed thumb and forefinger).

It is difficult to find a bottom-feeding species that will *not* be attracted to sea worms fished whole, in gobs, or in pieces. Bits of bloodworm, however, lose body juices quickly when soaked in sea water and only the skin will remain. While whole worms, properly streamed, are considered most enticing to a majority of big-mouthed game fishes, note that circumstances alter cases. Small chunks or lengths, although quick to bleach out, are best used on such small-mouthed species as scup. There, the use of the entire worm is wasteful: it will be nibbled off progressively instead of being taken in one quick gulp.

No matter what the scientific or local name may be, sea worms stand high in the ranks of preferred bait—as the retail price indicates all too clearly! Earthworms and terrestrial night crawlers in an emergency may be substituted for sea worms, but they die quickly when immersed in sea water, bleach to a sickly white, and all in all have little appeal to marine species.

A completely different class of baits are the crabs, found on all coasts and in many shapes and sizes. The swimming species, such as the blue and lady crabs, have flippers of a sort on the hindmost pair of legs, while the walking species, such as the green and fiddler crabs, are furnished with pointed rear legs to help them scuttle over land or the ocean floor. As far as fishermen are concerned, the crabs used most often for bait are those found in the littoral area where they may be taken in pots or traps, dipped up with a net when stalked at tide line, or even caught by lowering a chicken neck on a piece of string into tidal-creek waters. The greedy crustaceans don't think things through and will hold onto the neck until they are lifted on shore.

Normally claws are broken off these types of crabs when fished whole and the hook is driven through the rear of the carapace. The claw meat from larger species makes an excellent bait for small bottom feeders. If the fish sought has a mouth too small to engulf a whole crab, cut the bait into quarters, shell and all. Although a stout knife will do this job, we have found that a hacksaw blade is superior.

As crabs grow, they cast off their old shells, then hide as best they can until the new shells harden. Just before they shed, their condition may be determined by breaking off the flexible pincer of one of the large claws. If it breaks off easily, leaving meat exposed, the crab is a shedder or peeler, which makes an excellent bait. The old body shell may be pried loose and the new soft crab can then be served up whole or cut in pieces. After the shell has been shed naturally, the crab is known as a soft-shell and is a top-notch food for both humans and fish. However, soft-shells are difficult to find and they rarely venture into crab pots because in moving they are unprotected from their enemies. The term buckram is used for soft-shells that have started to harden and, here again, a crab in this condition is a preferred bait.

Fiddler crabs might be considered a special category. They burrow into sod banks and marshy flats, and a colony may consist of many hundreds. Although some bait shops stock fiddlers and their close cousins, soldier crabs, most anglers harvest their own either by digging them out with a clam rake or by driving them into a funnel-shaped net. The net opening can be extended to cover a larger area by placing pieces of driftwood at a 45 degree angle to the fixed netting.

A fiddler crab with its large claw removed—a fine bait for Atlantic tautog and sheepshead.

Hooking fiddlers may be done through the rear of the carapace as with other crabs, but a better way is to remove the large claw that gives the species its name and run the hook point through the exposed joint opening so that point and barb are exposed. Fiddlers make a prime bait for the sheepshead of the Atlantic and Gulf, and for the sheephead of the Pacific. Often they are crushed to use as chum for these species.

Another special category of crabs is the hermits. These are found on all coasts, normally between high and low water marks, and they take up residence in the vacated shells of snails, whelks, and the like. Few bait shops carry these regularly, so fishermen must find their own in tidal pools or along the shore at low tide. The shell should be cracked open, then the hook point passed through the hard head of the critter and the soft body meat threaded along the hook bend. The stubby claws may be removed if desired, but we prefer to leave them in place.

Crabs of all species may be kept for several days in a cool, darkened container with seaweed of any kind as bedding. They can be stored alive almost indefinitely in slatted bait cars submerged in salt or brackish water. Add a fish head or skeleton to feed them and keep them in good condition. Shedders and soft-shells should be kept separate from their cannibalistic friends or they will disappear in short order.

The sand bug or mole crab is the smallest practical bait found in quantity along open beaches on all coasts. Normally about an inch long, it burrows into the sand as a wave recedes, then pops out again to feed before another wave breaks on shore. A scoop net made with fine mesh is the most efficient tool to gather a supply of these tiny tempters. One or more may be impaled on a hook—and they will take pompano, palometas, Pacific croakers, and many other species. A fine wire hook is preferred, for heavy wire will shatter the light shell, and the bait will soak off almost immediately.

Among the crustaceans, the wide variety of shrimp species on all coasts are favorite baits. They range in size from the tiny grass shrimp, normally only about an inch in length, to the squilla or mantis shrimp—which is not a true shrimp—some of which grow to almost a foot. Terminology is confusing, for in many areas the terms shrimp and prawn are used interchangeably. Normally, the words designate size with the prawn the larger of the two.

Californian ghost shrimp—there are three major species—are equipped with a single claw. Like the squillas, they live in burrows set in sand or mud and may be dug out in much the same manner as clams or sea worms. Many of today's anglers employ a "plumber's helper" suction device that literally sucks them out of their burrows. These delectable—to a game fish—little shrimp are widely used, both in bottom fishing and when drifting. Although other species may dig themselves in temporarily, usually they are found feeding in eelgrass beds or similar concentrations of marine vegetation including seaweed clinging to underwater pilings. A fine-meshed dip net can be used to capture them. This method is particularly effective after dark in waters illuminated by a fixed light, such as one on a dock or pier. Cast nets and regular minnow seines are also effective for those who catch their own bait.

Small shrimps may be kept alive for 24 hours or more by placing them in a cooler on a tray made with a burlap or mesh bottom. Ice should be put at the bottom of the cooler and should *not* come in contact with the critters because fresh water shortens their life-span.

Cover the tray with sawdust, then add a light layer of shrimp, another of sawdust, and so on until capacity is reached. Top off the whole works with a piece of burlap soaked in sea water—and keep the cooler away from direct sunlight. This system of storage is often used by those who chum for species such as weakfish with grass shrimps or the transparent glass shrimps found among tidal grasses. Large shrimps are best kept alive in a regular bait car submerged in circulating salt water.

A few bait shops in areas where large shrimps are commonly used keep a live supply on hand in aerated tanks. However, most sell this bait either freshly dead or frozen. If there is any question concerning freshness, settle for the frozen. A shrimp loses its fresh appeal rapidly after death.

Vital organs in the head section of a large live shrimp will appear as a dark blotch when the crustacean is held to the light. A thin wire hook may be placed in the clear area just behind the eyes and the bait will survive for some time. It also may be hooked through the tail meat, yet will not swim naturally when this is done. Dead specimens may be hooked in the same manner, but we prefer to run the hook point through the forward part of the head, then thread it down through the tail meat. The tail will then curl in a natural manner over the hook bend. If the fish sought have small mouths, the peeled tail meat alone or in bite-sized pieces serves well. With grass and glass shrimps, several may be threaded on the hook by the head-to-tail method.

Although almost any game fish sought by anglers will feed on shrimp, there is a far wider category of bait available and used—the scores of bait fishes. As far as bottom fishermen are concerned, they range from tiny minnows to species like mackerel, which may be considered game fish in their own right. To discuss them in detail would fill a separate book, so a look at the general categories will have to suffice.

In tidal creeks and marshes along the entire Atlantic seaboard, in much of the Gulf of Mexico, and along the California coast, mummichogs, killifishes, sheepshead minnows—or whatever the local name may be—are found. Scientists group several species under the heading of *Fundulus*. All are similar in appearance with rounded tails and a single dorsal fin placed well back on the body. Happy in salt, brackish, or fresh water, these fish are extremely hardy and may be kept alive at

Hal Lyman sets a minnow trap in a tidal marsh to catch mummichogs, also called killifish or killies. They are an excellent bait.

least for a day in a container holding wet seaweed or burlap. A bait bucket or car, as long as it is not exposed to excessive heat or sunlight, will keep them lively for days on end.

Coastal bait shops sell killies throughout the fishing season and, along the eastern seaboard, they are a favorite live bait for many of the toothed flounders. They should be hooked either through the lips or just ahead of the dorsal fin. If dead, the best way to present them is by putting the hook point into the bait's mouth, then threading it up the shank with hook point and barb protruding by the anal fin. Rigged in

Three methods of hooking mummichogs. Left to right: through the lips when bait is alive; close to dorsal fin; through the body when the bait is dead.

this way, killies will spin in a current so a swivel should be tied in between a snelled hook and the line or leader. All of the *Fundulus* clan may be caught in minnow traps set in a tidal creek or marsh and baited with anything from crushed mussels to bread. Cast nets, seines, and dip nets may be used, but the trap involves the least effort.

Another group of small inshore bait fish found on all coasts is the silverside. Although there are many species, each may be distinguished by a bright, reflective band running along the lateral line. Terminology becomes confusing. In California, two species are known as jack smelt and top smelt even though they are no kin to the true smelt family. A third is the grunion, which spawns at night during full tides and is caught by the thousands along the sandy beaches. On the eastern seaboard, some term them spearing or sperling. All make good baits, although difficult to keep alive and rather soft. Several may be put on one hook by running the point through the eye sockets of each.

Silversides school densely and may be caught in minnow traps, drop and cast nets, and seines. Night hours are the best for harvesting them in quantity. Many bait shops sell them either iced or frozen. Freezing softens the already soft meat, so the iced specimens are preferred. As in the case of shrimps, there are few game fishes that do not munch on silversides at some stage of their lives.

Sand launces, known also as sand eels because of their long and skinny body structure, are an abundant bait fish in northern waters of both the Atlantic and Pacific. Although they range far offshore, anglers normally find them along open beaches where they will burrow into the sand with amazing rapidity. Far tougher than the silversides, they are still hooked one or more through the eye sockets simply because the body circumference is so small that a hook will tear it apart. Few bait shops stock launce on a regular basis, so fishermen usually dig their own supply at the surf's edge or take them with minnow seines, cast and drop nets. At times, windrows of this species will be driven high and dry by marauding game species and anglers can fill the bait box.

For some unknown reason, when fishes are feeding on launces, they rarely will look at any other type of bait. This is true whether the predator is a striped bass or one of the toothed flounders. It therefore pays to keep an eye out for schools of sand eels, which often may be spotted leaping clear of the water when attacked. Gather a supply by whatever means possible under such circumstances. They may be kept alive for some time in any container packed with seaweed wet with salt water.

Larger forage fish are the mullets, of which there are several species that look very much alike. They are found from Cape Cod to Brazil on the Atlantic side and from Los Angeles County to Chile in the Pacific. The West Coast species grows up to 15 pounds in weight, a veritable giant among the mullets. Most of those used for bottom fishing in the United States range from the young three or four inches long—known as finger mullet—to adults weighing a bit less than three pounds. The former may be fished whole, while the latter normally are steaked in chunks. Mullet strips may be used when a fluttering action is desired. It pays to scale mullet before cutting them up because the scales are large and may interfere with penetration of the hook point.

Mullets feed basically upon diatoms and algae, although they may be taken on a very small hook baited with dough. Traveling in tightly packed schools, they can be seen riffling calm water with individual fish leaping clear from time to time in bays and estuaries. A cast net is the ideal weapon for capturing them quickly and in quantity. Southern bait shops and commercial fishing docks usually have a fresh supply on hand. This species is difficult to keep alive unless a very large holding tank is available; therefore the market is primarily for fresh and frozen specimens. Wherever mullets are found, game fishes will also be found feeding on them. Within their range, whole, chunked, or cut in strips, they are among the most popular of baits.

Although somewhat oily, mullet cannot compare in that characteristic with menhaden, known also as pogy, fatback, mossbunker, or just plain bunker. Swimming in densely packed schools which give a coppery tinge to the water, this fish is found from the Canadian Maritimes to Brazil, but not on the Pacific Coast. It supports a major commercial fishery for meal and oil. Since the species is a plankton feeder, anglers normally take their supply by snagging them, using a cast net, a short gill net, or by buying them fresh or frozen from commercial sources.

This species may be kept alive for short periods in aerated bait tanks or buckets. When dead, the oily meat spoils quickly so it should be well refrigerated. Small menhaden may be fished whole, normally with the hook thrust through the body just in front of the dorsal fin. Larger specimens should be cut in chunks rather than strips because the meat is soft and strips tend to tear loose. Note also that one or more menhaden hearts impaled on a hook make an excellent bait for many bottom feeders. Ground bunker, which may be purchased frozen from many bait suppliers if the fisherman does not want to go through the messy procedure of grinding his own, makes a top-notch chum. Mix beach sand with it if the chum slick needs to run deep. A small handful of ground menhaden may be used as bait by tying it into a woman's hairnet and rigging the package on a hook.

Close cousins to menhaden are the many species of herrings found on all coasts. They are obtained and fished in much the same manner as bunkers. However, the meat is firmer and may be used successfully when cut in strips. Pacific anglers cut "plugs" from these species by slicing the whole fish diagonally just behind the head. Although used primarily when trolling with a dodger or flasher rigged ahead of the plug, this rig will take fish when drifting or mooching.

Confusion arises on the East Coast because small herrings are often called sardines even though the true sardine *(Sardinops caerulea)* is strictly a Pacific species. Rarely more than a foot in length, it is a favorite bait, both live and dead, on that coast. Taken primarily by seines, sardines are standard for party boats on which they are kept alive in large aerated tanks. Fished alive, they are usually hooked through the nose or through the flesh just forward of the tail. Dead, they may be fished whole, filleted in strips, or cut in chunks. It is advisable to scale the dead bait so that the hook point will penetrate readily.

Similar in outline, but smaller and with an underslung jaw, anchovies are used almost interchangeably with sardines in the Pacific. There are several related species found in the Atlantic from Maine to Brazil, but they have never become a very popular bait in that area primarily because the commercial source of supply is uncertain and other baits are more readily obtained.

There are many other herringlike species on all coasts which may be used for bait when there is a supply on hand. However, a completely unrelated species—the common eel—is found only on the Atlantic side. It spawns in the Sargasso Sea and young eels, known as elvers, make the long migration back to fresh-water streams. The females ascend these while the males remain in the estuaries until both sexes have matured and start their long journey back to the spawning grounds. The easiest way to catch eels is to set a pot, baited with mashed mussels, fish scraps, or even chicken entrails, in brackish water. They will live for a long time if kept cool and moist in seaweed or burlap. Do *not* keep them in a bait car or container holding other species, for the eels will eat their companions in short order.

Since eels thrive in both fresh and salt water, they may also be kept for many days in a bait bucket or box which has a mesh tray suspended in it. Put the eels in the container, then fill the tray with ice cubes or cracked ice. The cool drippings will keep them lively.

Fished live, eels may be hooked through the lips, through the lips and then through the eye sockets, or close to the tail. If hooked in the middle of the body, they will squirm around and make a terrible tangle of leader and line. To handle these slimy critters, use a cotton glove or rub a wet hand in beach sand to ensure a firm grip. Live eels are a favorite bait, particularly when night fishing, for striped bass, large weakfish, and bluefish.

As we have mentioned before regarding other baits, match the size of the eel to the size of the quarry's mouth. Many forget that an eel need not be whole to catch fish. Cut in chunks, it makes a tough bait for almost any species feeding at or near the bottom—and exudes its own oily chum slick. Dead eels may be stored for a long time packed in kosher salt or in a brine made from it. The odor of the brine-soaked specimens is powerful, but fish seem to like it—another exception to the fresh-bait rule.

A live eel hooked through the lips to keep it swimming.

Kosher salt, incidentally, is better than table salt for preserving any baits. If a brine solution is to be used, boil the water to kill any bacteria that may be lurking ready to start the decaying process. Pacific anglers often lay down fillets of bait fish in a wooden or plastic container with a 50-50 mix of kosher salt and sugar. The bottom of the container is lined with the salt-sugar mixture, then comes a layer of fillets, then the preservative again, and so on—finished off with a salt-sugar topping. If kept cool, fillets will last for many weeks when preserved by this method.

There are dozens of baits we have not mentioned, ranging from "bullheads" (small sculpins) of the California coast to strips of fluke belly or mackerel used to catch their own cannibalistic kind. The general rule is that a predatory fish will eat almost any living marine creature that won't eat it first. By opening up the belly of the first fish of the day and examining the contents, you may well get a clue to the preferred bait of the moment. If possible, duplicate the meal and offer it on a well-sharpened hook.

eight

DIAMONDS IN THE

DEPTHS

*A*lthough bottom fishermen tend to think only of natural bait when discussing their sport, artificial lures should not be neglected. These vary from the large Norway jigs weighing as much as a pound or more to tiny lead-head models weighing fractions of an ounce, from deep running plugs festooned with hooks to flashy attractors without any hooks at all, mounted ahead of a live baitfish.

One of the most popular artificials on all coasts is the lead-head jig. It is basically a hook around which metal is molded leaving part of the shank and all of the bend and barb free. The hook point rides upward to prevent fouling on bottom, and the eye normally is at the top of the head rather than at the leading edge. This permits imparting a hopping action to the lure by twitching the rod tip.

In early days, such jigs were often termed *bucktails,* because the dressing tied to the shank came from a deer's tail. Bucktail hair still makes an excellent decoration for attracting fish, since its buoyancy gives a "breathing" action to the lure, but modern science has moved into the picture. Crimped nylon strands and a great number of soft plastics fashioned in a variety of shapes have replaced bucktail to a

Ivon Woolner with trophy bluefish she caught deep jigging off Cape Cod in Massachusetts.

large degree. Nomenclature applied to the lure may range from barracuda to doodlebug, depending upon the geographical area of the coast. The fact remains that lead-head jigs take a wide variety of bottom feeders.

Shape of the head itself, particularly when offerings weigh an ounce or less, must be taken into consideration. A jig flattened vertically so that it looks like a bean standing on edge will sink rapidly while one flattened horizontally tends to flutter down through the water much more slowly. The latter type, however, will skim over eelgrass beds and the like without fouling. No type should be encumbered with heavy snaps or snap swivels since these kill lure action and add to weed problems.

Obviously some casting skill is helpful when presenting lead-heads to fish, yet the angler does not have to be an expert by any means. When drifting in a boat, for example, a short cast in the direction *toward which* the boat is moving is all that is required to keep the line from rubbing on the side or keel during the retrieve. Let the lure hit bottom, take up slack, twitch the rod tip at regular intervals while cranking in line, and continue the process until the lure is at or near the surface. Often even deep feeders will follow the hook right up to the boat's side before grabbing it.

A similar system may be used from bridges and piers—and just lowering the lead-head into the current and stripping line until the lure hits bottom will do the trick. If presented on the up-current side, the hook will travel under the structure. If on the down-current side, try to have the lure pass through the shadow cast by the bridge or pier. Sometimes the sun fails to cooperate in such an attempt.

Tipping a lead-head with a bait strip, pork rind, plastic worm, or one of the many soft plastic decorations now manufactured improves taking power. Such additions cut down on casting distance due to wind resistance, but, as noted above, distance normally is not a primary requirement. Remember that a lead-head rigged in this manner is far longer than the lead-head alone. Addition of a trailing hook, particularly in the case of a plastic worm, will convert a tail-nipper to a hooked fish.

Experimentation with lure color pays off. Normally in murky water, such as that found in many river estuary areas of the Gulf of Mexico, yellow is favored. White, alone or in combination with red, does well in the clear, cold waters of the Northeast. Pink is a favored hue in Florida's estuarine channels. Pacific anglers seeking rockfish lean toward black lead-heads tipped with black or purple plastic worms or twisty tails. The jig head itself may be of the same color as the dressing, but variations are the norm. Chrome-plated or stainless heads are particularly effective when fishing under bright sunlight. There is only one general rule that holds in all waters: if a color combination is not getting results, try another.

Metal spinners may be added to lead-heads to provide additional attracting powers. These are effective on many of the toothed flounders. Normally such spinners are mounted just in front of the head, yet a model used for rockfish on the Pacific coast, known as a tail-spin, has a bean-shaped head with painted eye and a small spinner attached to its rear by wire—replacing the usual bucktail, nylon, or plastic dressings.

Plastic worms, which have become very popular among fishermen seeking black bass in fresh and brackish waters, may also be used for marine species without benefit of a lead-head jig. The head of the worm should lie smoothly along the hook shank with the tail streaming astern. When very light tackle is used, a single split shot will give sufficient weight to the lure for it to reach bottom. Some crimp the shot right at the eye of the hook, basically converting the whole

Typical bottom fishing lures, top to bottom: Norway jig; diamond jig with tubing tail; basic diamond jig; slab-type jig with plastic tail; Scrounger, featuring an oscillating head and plastic tail adornment; Seven-Strand Clout.

offering to a miniature lead-head. Others prefer to place the weight three to six inches ahead of the hook on the leader. It will then ride along the ocean floor when drifting or casting, while the slightly buoyant plastic wiggles along in much the same manner as a natural sea worm. Clamp-on and drilled egg sinkers may be used in place of split shot when heavier tackle is employed.

Note that most fish when taking a plastic worm rarely gulp the lure down in a sudden rush. Therefore when the first touch is felt, drop the rod tip to allow a bit of slack line so that there is no strain on the hook itself. When the fish starts to move off, set the hook firmly. Tail-nippers may be taken by rigging a second trailing hook embedded in the plastic, but this prevents maximum action of the lure. When we miss short strikes, we console ourselves with the reflection that they are caused primarily by small fish.

Another type of lead-head and plastic combination that has become popular among bottom fishermen in recent years is of chunky design, similar in outline to a fat grub or small bait fish with or without a curled tail. Unlike plastic worms, these lures are usually gobbled down quickly by bottom feeders and the hook should be set quickly. The majority have interchangeable "tails" which are held in place snugged up against the metal head by scorings on the hook shank. One head-and-hook combination may be decorated with a variety of colors without disconnecting it from the leader or line. Bounced slowly over the bottom, such lures are effective on species ranging from seatrout to scup, from hake to halibut. Match the size to the size of the mouth of the fish sought.

Another type of artificial lure used widely in bottom fishing is the metal jig. Largest among these is the Norway that may weigh a pound or more. Using this chrome-plated monster is described in the chapter dealing with fishing methods, but basically the lure is simply lowered to the bottom, reeled in a foot or two, then moved rhythmically up and down by rod action. The fish comes to investigate the flashing metal, takes a cut at it, and is hooked either in the mouth or under the chin.

Such jigs are expensive but are favorites among New England anglers seeking cod, haddock, and cusk. Since these Yankees are noted for their parsimony, it would be expected that they would develop a cheaper, homemade substitute, but that development came from the Pacific when the pipe jig was born. Taking a piece of copper, stainless steel, brass, or aluminum pipe one-half to an inch in

DEEP-WATER JIGS

Norway jig   *Home-made pipe jig*   *Diamond jig*

diameter, place one end in a can half full of sand. Pour molten lead into the other end. When the lead cools, the pipe is cut into suitable lengths at a 45 degree angle to give the finished lure action. Holes may be drilled through the body of the jig, and a couple of treble hooks may be mounted on opposite sides by means of brass or stainless cotter pins. However, if the bottom is rocky or weedy, chances of fouling are high. A single or treble hook affixed by a split ring through a hole at one end of the lure reduces this problem. A snap swivel at the other end completes the picture. The pipe's finish may be buffed up with a pad of steel wool to shine enticingly, or the surface may be painted any desired color with a good quality marine enamel.

Diamond jigs, so named because of their shape in cross-section, normally run a bit lighter in weight than the Norway types. Most are chrome-plated and range in size from about eight to 14 ounces. For deep-water fishing, weight chosen will depend on both depth and current. The trick is to keep line from rod tiptop as nearly perpendicular as possible.

Always, where subsurface currents are strong, a belly in the line becomes a major handicap. There is drift, no matter the weight of the lure used, and this drift may be frustratingly rapid. Presently a point is reached where proper positioning is impossible: this occurs as swift current bellies and buoys a running line. The jig is wafted down-current and then is dragged *upward* away from a near-bottom strike zone. When this point is reached, feeding more line is hopeless; one simply retrieves and makes another drop.

One tactic is employed by anglers who have adequate room to execute a short to medium cast. From an anchored boat, throw the jig *up-current*. Under a following Dacron line it will then sink rapidly, will still be borne along by strong flow, but by the time bottom contact is felt it should be in ideal position to initiate perpendicular jigging.

Note that diamond jigs are not confined to deep-water fishing only: they may be purchased in sizes as small as a half-ounce and used with great success on species such as the common and Spanish mackerel on all coasts. As is true of other types of jigs, addition of a small cut bait strip, pork rind, or plastic tail sweetens the offering. Deep-water specialists like to add a fairly sizable strip to a jig's hook, both to exude scent and provide greater fluttering action. A minor handicap is that the strip adds a mite of water resistance and thus may speed down-current progress of a lure.

Countless other metal jigs are on the market. Many, such as the hammered-finish stainless-steel Hopkins No-Eql, were originally de-signed just for jigging use but today have developed into casting lures as well. Bottom fishermen can use any of these with a good chance of success. However, a model that is designed to move very erratically when drawn through the water on a horizontal plane tends to foul terminal tackle when jigged up and down on a vertical plane. A metal spoon, for example, may be used when drifting, with or without a sinker rigged a foot or more ahead of the lure. When jigged from a stationary platform—bridge, pier, or anchored boat—it has poor action and will tangle frequently.

A specialized rig for jigging and taking several fish at a time is often know as the Christmas tree. A regular bank sinker or any metal lure may be used to take the hooks down to the bottom. Above this weight, snelled hooks are tied into the leader so that they project at right angles. Some use short spreaders for this purpose, but in our opinion these encourage tangles. On each hook is a short section of rubber or plastic tubing, each approximately two inches in length for species such as the mackerel. Fluorescent plastic in yellow, red, or orange seems to get best results. Using more than six hooks makes the rig difficult to handle.

Double hook-ups, these on surgical tubing and jig, keep a party boat mate busy clearing line tangles.

The whole works is lowered to the bottom, then jigged *gently*. Violent jigging will produce a mare's nest of hooks and lures. If a fish is hooked, do not retrieve line immediately—just keep it taut, and often one or more others will join their companion. For reasons unknown, the short-tube lures appear to work far better than flies, plastic worms, or grubs. However, a single tube fished alone in this manner produces little. Whether the fish have figured that tubes of this type only travel in schools is anyone's guess.

One danger associated with use of the multiple-hook "tree" should be kept in mind. When a rig is "loaded" and brings four to six fish to the surface, your rod may be sharply bowed under the strain of accumulated weight. No big problem—unless, in the process of swinging a multiple catch aboard, two, three, or all manage to dislodge themselves and flop back into the brine. Immediately, the rod's spring tension is released, sharp hooks fly in all directions while anglers dodge. In working a Christmas tree, we advocate caution, plus the wearing of goggles to guard against horrifying eye injury.

Primarily on our Pacific coast, deep-water bottom fishermen employ a close cousin of the tree. It is correctly called a gangion and consists of multiple hooks tied in at intervals on a leader equipped with a suitable terminal weight. The major difference is that each hook is baited, rather than dressed as an artificial.

In the broad sense, attractors can be considered lures of a sort. As mentioned in the chapter concerning methods of fishing, the Jersey Doodlebug is among these. With a floating head on a hook, dressed with bucktail, it holds bait off the bottom out of reach of scavengers, yet gives the bait itself some motion in the current. Similarly, small plastic floats of various colors may be tied onto a leader just ahead of a baited hook for the same purposes. Surf fishermen along the coasts of the Carolinas and Virginia favor fluorescent models such as the Fireball when after bluefish, seatrout, and flounder. Such rigs also serve to save bait and attract fish when still fishing or drifting.

Fluorescence is one thing: luminescence is another. In the latter, light is actually given out from some source. Some years ago, big-game anglers seeking broadbill swordfish near the bottom in deep water discovered that Cyalume light sticks, rigged on the leader ahead of a natural bait, did great execution. The word spread and today this type of luminous lure is used by bottom fishermen under a wide variety of conditions from night fishing for hake in the depths off the coast of Maine to trolling up groupers and snappers from the clear waters of Florida.

In many cases, the light stick alone with a hook rigged close to one end of it is all that is required. However, chances are improved if a baited hook is placed several inches below the stick itself. Once activated, Cyalume will lose its effectiveness if exposed to bright sunlight and heat. Keep the stick in a bucket of cold water when moving from one fishing ground to another and its life will be extended. In the past, metal lures painted with luminous coatings never achieved popularity, perhaps because they were used primarily in shallow water. With the proven success of light sticks in the depths, anglers are now experimenting with luminous paints of various types and results may be very surprising.

In a completely different category of lures are plugs—one of the few types that originated in America. They come in all sizes, shapes, and colors, but only a relatively small number are of interest to bottom fishermen. The first group consists of those that are heavily weighted so that they sink immediately when they hit the water. Going back to fundamentals, one of the earliest quick sinkers was known throughout much of the South as the Clothespin and was used widely for taking seatrout. Hand crafted, it was shaped much like a small clothespin with the forward section made of lead and the rear of wood. Today, its closest cousin is the Porter Sea Hawk, which is really a metal jig rather than a true plug. The general shape of the old clothespin type, however, has been retained.

Regular quick-sinking plugs for the most part have less violent action than surface or subsurface models. They are designed to run deep and rather slowly. Although some added action may be given to the lure by raising and lowering the rod tip smartly, this often may be considered a waste of effort when plumbing depths of 40 feet or more. If the line used is monofilament, its elasticity will neutralize rod action to a large degree. However, if drifting over a known deep spot in an otherwise level bottom, dropping the rod tip so that the lure dips into the hole or channel may well entice a bottom feeder from its hidey-hole. This technique is particularly effective when seeking snappers and groupers in tropical and semitropical waters. As aforesaid, other than in shallow to semi-medium depths, Dacron is a far more efficient line than monofilament. Often wire is even better to help get a lure down into payoff territory, and nowadays there is increasing use of the down-rigger.

In addition to the quick-sinking plugs are those which range from neutral buoyancy to slow sinking. To get to the depths, these depend upon a large lip angled downward. As the lure is drawn through the water, pressure on the lip causes it to dive. Within reasonable limits, the higher the speed of retrieve, the deeper it will plunge. Some anglers have honed presentation of such plugs to a fine art. Taking advantage of currents on a drift, when anchored or when fishing from a shore structure, they can maintain the level of the lure just a foot or two off bottom while reeling in line very little, if at all. These plugs vibrate far more rapidly as a general rule than the quick sinkers and may draw game species from a considerable distance.

Even floating plugs may be used effectively when bottom fishing. The trick here is to add a sinker heavy enough to drag the lure down. The weight should be on the leader from 18 to 24 inches ahead of the plug's eye. Keel sinkers help to prevent spinning and twisting. The sinker may touch the ocean floor from time to time, but the plug and its hooks will ride above most obstructions and its action will be impaired very little.

Although plugs weighing more than two ounces are favored by those seeking large underwater cave dwellers, like the snappers and groupers already mentioned, they should not be ignored by fishermen after smaller game. Almost any species that feeds on live bait fish may be taken on these lures. Changing pace by offering a plug when other artificials fail to produce may crown failure with success.

Undoubtedly artificial lures of any kind will not replace natural bait among bottom fishermen on all coasts. However, including them in the fishing weapons system gives an angler a better chance of joining the group of allegedly lucky experts whose luck is really based on superior skills.

nine

BASIC

ACCESSORIES

*A*ll salt-water anglers require some accessories to complement their
regular tackle, but bottom fishermen face some special problems
in selecting such gear. Although most of our bottom-bouncers do not
carry a wide assortment of lures, (sometimes most perceptive of them)
what they *do* tote to the sea may be heavy, like sinkers and dead or live
bait. Remember these requirements when selecting a tackle box.

Such boxes come in a wide variety of designs. Obviously, models
that are impervious to the ill effects of salty corrosion should be
chosen. Most of the standard types boast one or more compartmented
trays to accommodate lures at top level, together with a comparatively
open bottom level to store a spare reel or other large item. If sinkers
are placed in the lure compartments, then the box may become top-
heavy and it will tend to tip over when fully opened. Jumbling sinkers
together at the bottom of the box may well result in damage to
neighboring non-sinker gear and, in addition, the sinkers pile up in
one corner if the box is tilted. The problem may be solved by packing
sinkers by size into individual plastic containers before stacking them
at deck level.

Adding a couple of dead mullets to the mix results in a messy disaster; usually any natural bait is best carried separately. For years beyond our count many bottom fishermen, particularly those who frequent piers and bridges and the high surf, have stooped to conquer and have simply utilized a pail in which to carry their gear. Initially this was a wooden bucket, then it got to be a galvanized pail. In either case, rigged hooks were (for that matter, still are) hung inside around the rim of the bucket, and bait was dropped into the bottom of the container.

The basic and logical design is honored, but—like all good things rediscovered—a measure of sophistication has been built in. Galvanized pails are still used, even though they tend to rust after a while. Sturdy wooden buckets are simply no longer available for that most economical of prices—nothing! It was different when grandfather was a boy; then lard and butter and a host of other foodstuffs were delivered in stout wooden containers made by journeymen coopers.

Today, bottom fishing specialists progressively go to hard plastic pails which are stamped out on an assembly line and considered expendable after use by such as the peddlers of ice cream. On certain sections of the seacoast these heretofore discarded containers are now scrounged up so fast that they almost appear to be an endangered species. The game's the same, although some alterations in original design are apparent.

The trick is to acquire a hard plastic bucket or pail large enough to accommodate basic terminal tackle and bait, one with a tough, clamp-on cover—although a lot of home craftsmen find it necessary to make their own covers. Instead of hanging hooks and rigs from the rim, a circular disk is epoxied an inch or so below the cover seat, and this is drilled to secure hooks. It is functional, neat, and clean. Otherwise, nothing much has changed.

With this arrangement hooks will not slide around as they do on a metal edge. A screen mesh tray may be installed to keep bait from mixing with other essentials and, if you're a sissy—as we are—it's easy to pad the cover for *easy* sitting. In some areas custom-made buckets of this type, complete with foam-padded seats, are now marketed by smart old entrepreneurs with salt-wet feet. You can still make your own without a degree in engineering.

Carrying dead bait is neither a tidy nor easy job. Some favor heavy duty plastic bags such as those used for freezing foodstuffs. We have never found a way to seal these perfectly and, after a short time, malodorous liquids seep out to taint everything in their proximity. Plastic freezer boxes do a better job and the tops stay on unless subjected to unusual punishment. Plastic jars with screw tops serve well. Glass can be used, but is inevitably subject to breakage. Our suggestion is to avoid glass, for you are never going to know the definition of unholy stink until you bust one of those brittle beauties and spill out a bunch of tired squid or other one-time delicacies of the sea temporarily forgotten. In any event, whether the jug is glass or plastic, metal screw-tops should be anointed with a coat of grease because they tend to corrode quickly when exposed to salt moisture.

A bait board upon which to cut up herring, mullet, or other bait fish comes in handy—since suitable pieces of driftwood never seem to be around when needed for this purpose. (The wooden cover of the plastic bucket aforementioned is one choice.) A short length of wood fastened with epoxy to the top of a tackle box is often favored and, if the box is big enough, one edge of this strip can be scribed as a ruler to measure questionable legal length of fish brought to account.

Do *not* get fancy and coat this chopping block with paint, since the enamel will soon peel off in big-league use. Virgin wood is clean: scour it after each sentimental journey, and don't worry about status nonsense. Professionals demand the most utilitarian of tools and they rarely paint lilies.

For live bait that does not have to keep swimming, such as sea worms, shrimps, clams, crabs, and the like, an insulated bait canteen is a good investment. These come in a variety of shapes and sizes, each normally featuring a mesh tray to keep the bait clear of whatever coolant may be used. Drippings of fresh water will kill many of these species so, except in the case of eels—as noted elsewhere—ice should be placed at the bottom of the container with the bait safely racked above.

Ice, block or crushed, lasts a comparatively short time, and we favor the sealed plastic containers filled with a glycerin compound which is available at small cost from supermarkets and hardware stores. Placed in a deep-freeze or the ice compartment of a refrigerator overnight, they will remain frozen for as long as 72 hours. By all means introduce your wife to the joys of angling, else she may get migraine headaches about good, clean bait tucked under the human staff of life. Properly packaged, there is no threat. Easily cleaned with a wet cloth, sealed containers also have the advantage of exuding no liquids.

Packing materials will vary with the baits used. Sawdust moistened with salt water is standard for shrimps, although if you want to keep them vibrantly alive a small bait car is necessary. If shrimps are to be used in chumming, as well as for bait, add uncooked rolled oats to the mix. The oat granules flutter down through the water, reflect light, and add appeal to the chum line. Use seaweed or Irish moss for sea worms; nothing at all for crabs, other than *coolth* (a word we just invented) and slight moisture.

In the case of swimming live baits, boat fishermen enjoy an advantage. Wells built right into the cockpits of large hulls will keep the swimmers happy. Note that circular wells, or those with rounded corners, are to be preferred over those with rectangular conformation. These last cause ever-swimming bait fishes to become trapped, to bash themselves against the corners and thus sustain injury. Pacific party-boat operators have developed the best live-bait containers in the world, most mainly above waterline with individual circulating systems. A quick aside: never use marine anti-fouling paint to coat a bait well or container of any sort; the metallic salts released from these will turn most fish belly-up in short order.

For small craft, a variety of portable live wells are available. These range from a Styrofoam floating ring to be hung over the side or transom to plastic tanks with their own water circulating systems. Over-the-side models may also be home-crafted from soft wood and plastic netting.

For the shore-based angler, choices are limited. Aerated buckets that have a small hand pump built into them work in a limited way, but we have yet to see one that will stand up well after much exposure to sea water. The floating net bag, mentioned above, or a similar bait car may be used from a bridge or pier and, with difficulty, from the beach. Once lowered into the briny, such devices will keep bait fish lively. The difficulty is getting the bait to the car in the first place. A regular bucket is the normal vehicle, yet if the distance to be covered is great, many of the fishlets will expire before reaching their destination. There is no easy solution other than catching bait right at the scene of angling action.

For cutting up bait, cleaning fish, trimming the ends from knots in fishing line, and for a dozen other tasks, a quality knife is one accessory no fisherman should be without. Small sheath knives are preferred on the oceanfront because human fingernails soften in salt water—which makes the opening of a clasp knife a major task. In days gone by, stainless-steel knives would not take or keep a keen edge. This is no longer true, as is made evident by stainless razor blades. Filleting knives, which feature fairly thin, long narrow blades, are the choice of most because they serve all purposes. A honing stone or one of the newer (and more costly) sharpeners like the Brass Rat and Neivert Whittler should be in your tackle box or belted around your waist. Although any of these may be used for sharpening hooks, a small bastard file kept in a watertight container serves this purpose better, especially if the object is to triangulate large hooks.

Another almost indispensable piece of equipment is a pair of pliers. On the Pacific and Gulf Coasts, fishermen appear to favor needle-nosed types with wire-cutting edges at the base of the jaws. These models double in brass as hook disgorgers. Along the Atlantic seaboard, most select pliers with parallel-moving jaws and the wire-cutters on the outer edge of the jaw. Construction of these pliers allows them to serve as a small wrench to tighten up loose reel nuts and the like. Choice is purely a matter of personal preference, for both serve their purposes well. Indeed a hearty number of anglers like to have both types on or about their persons during a fishing trip.

In a completely different category are nets, gaffs, and clubs. Although many of the smaller bottom-caught species can be swung aboard a boat or slid up onto the beach, a landing net will save many soft-mouthed species, such as seatrout, which are apt to tear free when lifted from the water. The obvious rule is: the larger the fish, the larger the net. Nylon mesh is preferred over cotton, since nylon does not rot out. When fishing from a high-sided boat, a long-handled net is the choice, but such models are awkward to use from smaller craft.

Pier and bridge fishermen sometimes use nets with tremendously long handles to reach the water surface, but these are difficult to maneuver. In their place, a fairly shallow net with no handle at all does a better job. No handle, because it is rigged at the end of a stout cord and lowered into the water by a companion so that it rides just below the surface. The angler then leads his catch over the rig, which is hoisted quickly to lift the fish high and dry. Incidentally, this system of bringing the fish to the net, rather than the net to the fish, is standard procedure no matter what the circumstances may be. Swiping at a catch in its native element with water-logged webbing is an invitation to failure.

In general, gaffs are used by few bottom fishermen unless the quarry is unusually large. However, a light and sharp gaff can be a better landing weapon than a net when fishing from a jetty or shore structure where rocks abound. There, wet mesh is inclined to foul as waves surge in. Here, again, the catch should be led over the gaff point before it is driven home. Slashing around like a tropical islander cutting sugar cane will result in a parted leader or line more often than not. Some surfmen employ a short-handled gaff to aid in beaching fish: we prefer to ride the catch ashore on an incoming wave and then, if it remains rambunctious, to tap it on the noggin with a short club.

Before leaving the subject of gaffs, there is also the "bridge gaff," which is often three- or four-pronged and lowered to a payoff location exactly as is the bridge net, and then driven home at an optimum moment when a tired quarry has been brought to the surface. These grapnels are most often employed where fairly large fish must be lifted vertically by an angler fishing off a bridge span. They are effective, barring the fact that a good many near-beaten warriors—although mortally wounded—tear loose. The rig will work anywhere and, although it is not likely to be hailed a very sporting tool, it is a means to an end.

So is the club. Or, as some classic angling literature would have it, a "priest." There is nothing much better to subdue a thrashing gamester in a small boat or for zapping a middle-heavyweight after it has been planed ashore on a ground swell. The club need not be fancy or custom-made: buy an adze handle, drill a hole in the grip and thread some light bungee cord through it. Sling the thing around your neck and it will be no burden, but it will be there when you need it for joyous mayhem. Of course clubs and gaffs placed other than in the cartilaginous jaws of fish are sort of lethal. If release is the order of the day, don't use them.

When *Salt Water Sportsman* was spawned back in 1939 the trademark logo was a surf caster with a towel dangling from his belt leaning into a fish. Times change, yet some things endure. A terry cloth towel still serves its purpose, in handling both slippery baits and sharp-spined catches. Rinse it out now and then, when there is time between tides, and it won't smell too bad.

Surely you have not forgotten to tote a flashlight after dark? Depending on need, this may be nothing more than a penlight which can be tucked in an inner shirt pocket under foul-weather gear, or a miner's headlamp. Having established a location to work through the night hours, a bright propane or gasoline lantern may draw bugs from the next three counties—but it will also attract small bait and the predators on their tails. Steadily burning lights do not seem to alarm game fishes, although many of them are spooked by flashes out of the dark.

There are countless other accessories available to bottom fishermen, and they range from sunscreen lotion and insect repellent to supermarket carts used by pier anglers as carryalls, from binoculars to a few Band-Aids tucked away with the scarce dollar bill in a wallet. The aim is efficiency and comfort, sans excess weight. Our advice is to keep the burden of such gear to the minimum necessary for effective fishing. Man is resilient and there is always a measure of combat in any high-level endeavor.

The obvious exception applies to boatmen, who should carry *all* life-saving and navigational equipment required by Coast Guard regulations. This exception may not add to your catch, but it will better your chances of survival. The sea is a playground; it is also a watery graveyard for stupids.

INDEX

Numbers in italics indicate information in illustrations.